W9-BXD-586

SILENT SONS

A Book for and About Men

Dr. Robert J. Ackerman

A Fireside Book
Published by Simon & Schuster
New York   London   Toronto   Sydney

F

FIRESIDE
Rockefeller Center
1230 Avenue of the Americas
New York, New York 10020

First Fireside Edition 1994

FIRESIDE and colophon are registered trademarks
of Simon & Schuster Inc.

Designed by Irving Perkins Associates
Manufactured in the United States of America

13 15 17 19 20 18 16 14

Library of Congress Cataloging-in-Publication Data
Ackerman, Robert J.
Silent sons: a book for and about men / Robert J. Ackerman.
p. cm.
Includes bibliographical references.
1. Adult children of dysfunctional families—United States—
Rehabilitation. 2. Men—United States—Psychology. 3. Adult
children—United States—Psychology. 4. Codependency—United
States. 5. Adjustment (Psychology)—United States. I. Title.
HV1441.8.U5A25   1993
362.82′4—dc20   93-26792
CIP

ISBN-13: 978-0-671-77537-7
ISBN-10:   0-671-77537-5
ISBN-13: 978-0-671-89286-9 (Pbk)
ISBN-10:   0-671-89286-X (Pbk)

Questions from *Is AA for You?* are reprinted
with permisson of Alcoholics Anonymous World Services, Inc.

To my father,
who changed silence into love

Contents

Preface

This book is for and about men who search for health as men. It is about men who experienced pain as boys growing up in dysfunctional families and survived it. They appear to be fine, but they carry their pain around quietly wherever they go. I call such men, including myself, "silent sons."

We would all like to change, and we don't need to be clinically diagnosed with a personality disorder to want to do this. We need only the desire to improve the quality of our lives.

This book is based on a national study of men conducted over the course of two years. It includes research data and extensive interviews that I conducted with more than 400 men from thirty-eight states, approximately 300 of whom came from dysfunctional families. I also interviewed over 100 silent sons who represent different types of dysfunctional families. These interviews were intensive and reveal the feeling, emotions, and insights that data alone could never impart.

This book is also for those who love us. It will help those who want to understand us better and love us more—our parents, friends, partners, lovers, siblings, or children who know that there is more to us than what we show them, more to us than what we *do*. If you want to know what we are, listen to us as we try to listen to ourselves and the voices of other men. Everyone thinks they understand what men are supposed to *be*, but few, including men themselves, really understand who men *are*.

I also interviewed over 100 women, each of whom is or was in a relationship with a silent son either as a mother, spouse, lover, sibling, or friend. I've included them to allow men to hear what women really say about them. Sometimes others see things we can't.

As you prepare to read this book, there are several things about silent sons and men's issues I would like you to keep in mind. I am not a defender of masculinity. I will not excuse anything and everything that men do. I do not profess that men are trapped by their past and incapable of change. But I will not engage in "male bashing" either. Too many dysfunctional families and systems have already done this.

I do not see silent sons as victim/blamers—that is, people who see themselves as victims and constantly blame others for their condition. Most silent sons are survivors, and the last thing they see themselves as (if they see themselves at all) is as victims. This book is also *not* an indictment of our parents. There is a big difference between trashing parents and looking for growth. This difference will be respected. Finally, this book will not "dysfunctionalize" everything. Contrary to popular myths, not every problem a silent son has originates with a dysfunctional family. Many of our issues come from simply being parents, spouses, workers, and men.

There are many positive attributes common among men raised in dysfunctional families. We are highly adaptable. We have great potential for growth and change. Silent sons share many bonds, not only with each other and other men, but also with women. And there is great diversity among silent sons. We are not all the same, and the ways in which we have been affected depend upon the type of dysfunctional family that we grew up in, the degree of the "emotional scarring" we experienced, the availability of outside support, and other factors such as cultural considerations and whether or not we received or sought any help.

I believe we are survivors who are capable of redefining ourselves and finding balance in our lives. We can appreciate being male; we can appreciate where we have been; and most importantly we can appreciate what we are capable of becoming. I see us challenging the "narrowness" of what it means to be a male. I see our potential.

This book is divided into four parts. The first part defines being male and examines how our identities and ideas developed not only as men, but also as boys raised in dysfunctional families.

The second part of the book explores the impact our parents have had on us. It examines how we struggle with accepting a dysfunctional mother or father. The most powerful of all our relationships, father and son, leads us to a closer look not only at ourselves but also at our fathers and at their pain and their influence on us. Each man needs to understand his parents in order to make the necessary separations from them to become his own man.

The third part of the book explores how our past has affected our relationships with other men, with women, with co-workers, and with our children. The core of all of our relationships is intimacy, but we need to ask ourselves: How do we as men define it, and how do we live it? This section also contains the chapter about what women have to say about us.

The last part of the book is about achieving our potential. It is about trading in old tapes for new songs and becoming healthy men. It is about silent sons coming together in a common search to define manhood and to redefine ourselves. It is about awakening to the possibilities in our lives.

My study of this subject began in the 1970s when I started working as director of an alcohol and drug rehabilitation program for the United States Army. In addition to working with addicts, I worked with children and adults who were raised in dysfunctional families, especially those raised in alcoholic families. Like so many of the people I encountered, I too came through difficult times in my life, including abuse, adoption, parental alcoholism, and my own divorce. In 1978 I wrote the first book in the United States on children of alcoholics and had the privilege of being a cofounder of the National Association for Children of Alcoholics. Since then I have worked as a university professor, author, lecturer, and consultant to all types of family programs throughout the United States and other countries. My work has allowed me to meet many more people from dysfunctional families and to not only hear their pain, but also watch them change and overcome difficult times in their lives.

In the last ten years the large numbers of people coming together in order to change and become healthier, to live better physically, emotionally, and spiritually, have started a recovery movement. But conspicuously absent from this movement have been men and men's issues.

In the earlier days when I did seminars and lectures, consistently 90 percent of my audiences were women. Women made up 80 to 90 percent of those in dysfunctional family support groups. Where were the men, I wondered? What do sons from dysfunctional families do with their pain, their feelings, their potential? Did someone put up a "Men Keep Out" sign, or did we put it up ourselves?

However, slowly but surely, men are becoming involved with the recovery movement. It is with great joy that I say to all silent sons, "Our time has come." The movement is here; the mentors are here; we are here. It is time to break the silence—not with anger, rage, fear, or despair, but with honor—and to break it by listening. The anagram of "silent" is "listen." We need to listen to those who have gone before us, and also to ourselves.

As you read this book listen to all the voices, including your own. Hear your potential, power, passion, and pain. Honor where you have been. Honor the boy inside. Honor the man who has survived. Honor the man you will become. Honor yourself.

SILENT
SONS

CHAPTER ONE

Are You a Silent Son?

> *A long habit of not thinking a thing wrong gives it the superficial appearance of being right.*
> THOMAS PAINE

A silent son is a man who grew up in a dysfunctional family, denies he was negatively affected by the experience, and continues to have problems in his life today. He might come from a family that coped with violence, alcoholism, compulsive gambling, child abuse, verbal abuse, workaholism, divorce, extreme rigidity, or a variety of other problems. The problems that he has in his life today could include an inability to maintain relationships, an inability to control anger, a tendency toward workaholism or addiction, fear of intimacy, violent behavior, or low self-esteem, to name just a few.

Some of the dominant characteristics of a silent son are:

- He keeps things that bother him to himself.
- He denies that unpleasant events occur.
- He fears letting people know him.
- He has difficulty interacting with his parents, spouse, or children.
- He has a strong fear of criticism.
- He is angry.

- He can't express his feelings.
- He disproportionately fears failure.
- He is obsessively driven to succeed.
- He desperately wants his life to be better but doesn't know how to change.

A silent son is a man in pain, but he doesn't want to admit it or allow anyone to see it. The pain is always present. He tries to ignore it. He tries to forget it. He becomes so involved in his career that he becomes convinced that the pain doesn't matter anymore. He surrounds himself with people whom he won't let get close to him, and he pretends that he belongs. But when he is alone or alone with his thoughts, he realizes the pain is still there.

What do you do when you are reminded of the pain of your childhood? Do you vow to forget it by doing whatever you can to distract yourself? Do you deny it or condemn it? A silent son may try to drink it away, work it away, romance it away, or tell himself that it doesn't get in his way.

It is not easy to admit that you are a silent son. You may believe admitting it makes you less of a man, less successful, strong, or competent than you appear. When it comes to your identity, you are a man first and a silent son second—however, it can be a very close second. Each influences the other. You *do not* give up being a man because you are a silent son. Likewise, you do not give up your positive feelings about your masculinity when you admit that you were raised in a troubled family.

Many of us are hesitant to admit that we came from a dysfunctional family because we fear exposure of our identity, we believe our past is a weakness, we prefer to avoid confronting our image of our parents, or we are merely following the philosophy that "life's tough" and so are we. Sometimes I wonder if we think it's easier to maintain our image than to maintain our health. A tree can be dead on the inside as long as two years before it begins to show on the outside. We can die on the inside too, long before they bury our remains.

Being a silent son does not mean that you are totally devastated or that you are incapable of doing healthy or successful things. A silent son doesn't always exhibit personality disorders, nor is he necessarily

16

"co-dependent," nor must he live in "shame." These problems *can* exist, but each silent son is entitled to his own emotional evaluation before someone tries to dismiss him as dysfunctional just because of his family background. A silent son may be in pain, but he can also have many positive characteristics. Some of these may include:

- He is good under pressure.
- He is adventuresome.
- He is independent.
- He is a survivor.
- He is empathic.
- He is a hard worker.
- He is a loyal friend.
- He is willing to help others.
- He is a problem solver.
- He has a good sense of humor.

> *Sometimes I have mixed feelings about being my dad's son. Then I realize I would not be the person I am if it were not for all of my experiences.*
>
> BRIAN

Regardless of outward appearances, most silent sons represent paradoxes. This does not mean that silent sons are totally out of balance. In fact, they often appear to others as if they "have it all together."

To better understand why this is so, it helps to examine the meaning of the word "dysfunctional." *Dys* comes from Latin and can be translated to mean pain. *Functional* means the ability to perform or function. When I talk about dysfunctional people, I am talking about people who are functioning in pain. Are they able to perform? Yes. Are they in pain? Yes.

One of the most intriguing paradoxes I see in some silent sons, especially adult sons of alcoholics, is a very high level of social skills in the presence of depression and low self-esteem. Most people who have clinical problems with self-esteem and depression are not usually capable of high levels of social functioning. But silent sons know

17

the right things to do socially even though they are hurting. Perhaps that is why they have been overlooked for so long.

Another common paradox involves self-defeating behaviors. A self-defeating behavior is any behavior that keeps you from living up to your potential or results in self-inflicted pain. It can include such things as procrastination, anger, fear, denial of feelings, inability to express your needs, or inability to stand up for yourself. Most self-defeating behaviors are learned in dysfunctional situations. The paradox is that at the time they are learned they don't appear to be self-defeating, but are seen as necessary for survival. When you are no longer in a dysfunctional situation and you continue to use these behaviors, negative outcomes result.

Paul, age 37, works as a carpenter. He grew up in an alcoholic family. He was afraid to say anything about what bothered him in his family as a child for fear that it would upset his mother. If he upset his mother she drank even more, and his father left the house when his mother drank. So Paul kept quiet. Silence was a behavior he learned in order to protect himself. However, today he confesses he is lonely and has a hard time opening up to people. His silence no longer works for him, but against him. It has become a self-defeating behavior. He is trying to break his old patterns of not speaking up for himself and isolating himself from other people. After almost totally secluding himself from others, he has finally joined a men's group, but he admits that at first he just sat there and listened. He was afraid to speak up. Paul states, "It's real tough. I think it's the feeling that I've had down in my heart for other people that I haven't been able to express. I've always wanted to be around other people and I've always wanted to reach out to them. Because inside I really do love other people . . . but it's just been very hard for me to do that."

INDICATORS OF SILENCE

The most common problem I find among silent sons is their belief that they're just like everybody else. In other words, many either believe that their family was not dysfunctional (when in fact it was) or believe that it was dysfunctional, but they were not affected. This is not unusual for men. The following are some classic behavior patterns in silent sons.

18

LIMITED EXPRESSION

Limited expression is the most significant of all the indicators of silence. One of the "male bashing" statements I often hear is that "men don't have emotions." Believe me, we have emotions! Visit any hospital and see how many men are hospitalized for stress-related disorders such as heart attacks, stomach problems, or addictions. The problem is, most men don't *express* their emotions.

It is stressful being a man, but even more so when you lack emotional expression. For example, consider the following facts:[1]

- The annual death rate from cancer for men is nearly one and one-half times higher than for women.
- Death rates from heart diseases are twice as high for men as for women.
- The ratio of ulcers in men versus women is 2 to 1.
- Divorced males' death rate is three times that of divorced women.
- Men are four times more likely than women to be the victims of murder.
- The rate of successful suicide is three times as high for men as for women.
- Men are the victims of on-the-job accidents at least six times more often than women.
- Men are thirteen times more likely to be arrested for drunkenness than women.
- Men live on the average seven years less than women.

Men are capable or expressing a wide range of emotions, but unfortunately they only allow themselves to do so in rare instances—at a game, for example. One of the most watched men's events is the Super Bowl. Here are grown men who personify the American male image of "big strong men," playing what is supposed to be a "game." Those who do well get very emotional. They jump up and down, openly hug each other, and dance in the end zone by themselves or with any available equally emotional partner. When the game is over, the winners continue with their tremendous release of emotions. The losers cry, hang their heads, and wear their emotions openly on their

19

faces and bodies. They are fully aware that millions of people are watching them, and still they allow their emotions to surface. The same can be said for the men in the stands (or at home watching the game on television), who often live vicariously through the game.

Expressing emotions and sharing them, however, are often two different things for men. Positive emotions are often shared, while negative ones are dealt with in solitude. Unlike joy, pain is seldom shared with other men. A team can express success, but when the team fails, the pain of failure is felt individually. Each man retreats inside himself. He does not turn to other men for solace.

The silent son knows he has emotions, but he doesn't know how to let them out. His inability to express himself is caused by various factors. He may simply not know how. He may not be able to correctly identify his emotions and may be trying to sort through them before articulating them. He may believe that emotions can only be expressed where it is socially acceptable or emotionally safe. He may be able to express emotions only with other men, or only with women. The problem is that those emotions which are not expressed are likely to show up in other, often negative, ways.

THE STRONG SILENT TYPE

We have all heard people describe some men as the "strong silent type." In fact, this is often said with admiration. It is as if people are saying that nothing affects this man, that he is always strong.

Have you ever wondered why the words "strong" and "silent" are put together? Are these two adjectives complementary? Do they mean that if you are silent you are strong, or that to be strong you must be silent? Or do they mean that we don't know what to do with pain other than be quiet? Maybe these words should be considered non sequiturs. I am not against being strong, but who says you can't talk or share *and* still be strong? The truly strong man not only knows *when* to ask but also *how* to ask for help.

Of course, like all men, I don't feel comfortable telling people everything about me. There are just some things you want to keep to yourself. There are some things you *should* keep to yourself. Besides, sometimes it depends on who is listening. But there is a difference between positive and negative silence. There is much to be said for the solitude of thought. There is much to be said for knowing when to keep your mouth shut. You *can* be alone with your thoughts, but you need not be a lonely man.

Negative silence is the silence of a man in pain. Negative silence tells you that you are being the "wrong" silent type. Your silence keeps you locked in and others locked out. Your loyalty to an image and to your silence demands a high price. The silent son makes his monthly payments loyally, but he's never paid up; the quieter he becomes, the more he owes.

THE SILENT TREATMENT

Do you know when you are giving those around you the silent treatment? I'll bet you do, but you won't admit it. We can give people the silent treatment for many reasons, but usually it is because we are upset about something. We can't or won't communicate our feelings; we resent that others don't sense our needs, and then we shut them out.

The silent treatment forces others around us to live in silence. They perceive that we are not only silent, but also unwilling to hear what they have to say. Our silence tells them they are not important to us. They are forced to adjust to our silences and learn to be silent around us. This is exactly how we, as the recipients of the silent treatment, learned it in our dysfunctional families. Now, as adults, we perpetuate the problem. As a result, needs are not met, resentments grow, and the silence runs deeper. The silent treatment can be very frustrating to us, not to mention the effect it has on others. Most of us know when we are doing it; few of us know how to stop it.

> *I buried my feelings for years, but if a feeling is strong enough it will eventually surface. My family has paid the price.*
>
> CLAY

21

Target Practice

The opposite of the silent treatment is taking out our frustrations on others, who become targets of our internal struggles. It means that instead of dealing with what is really bothering us, we project our negative feelings, usually anger, on others. We are the ones who are upset and we know that something is wrong. But instead of discussing our feelings, we attack others who can only guess at the real problem. Some guess better or question more directly than others. Some targets see what we are doing and reject or resent our assaults. Have you ever heard: "Don't take it out on me"? If so, you have been engaging in target practice.

The Imposter Syndrome

Do you ever feel like an imposter? Do you ever feel that even when you are doing well, you really aren't that good? Do you ever feel if people really knew all about you, they wouldn't like you? If so, you can identify with the imposter syndrome.

Feeling like an imposter reminds us that we are not what we appear to be. It creates an emptiness inside and makes us feel "hollow." All around us we hear others saying, "Be yourself." What we hear from ourselves is, "Be anything but yourself."

> *I believe I was led to think I should be something I was*
> *not. Don't feel, just do a good job. In working to break*
> *the cycle, I have found a very different person from the*
> *one I presented for so long.*
>
> Ken

At the core of the imposter syndrome lies low self-esteem, a feeling of unworthiness and the belief that appearance comes first and substance, second. We don't believe that people will like us for who we are. We don't believe that we are good enough. So being anyone other than ourselves must be an improvement. Remember as boys we would always pretend to be someone (or something) else? We would even argue over who got to be a certain hero and why. These heroes were bigger than life, bigger than us, but we were small, so that was OK. Playtime is over, yet many of us are still pretending. It's no fun anymore. And it only keeps us small.

It is very difficult to be an imposter. You feel like a phony and at the same time you resent your own charade. What's worse is not knowing how to stop pretending. It is difficult to be yourself when even you don't like what you have to offer. You feel that the you on the inside and the you on the outside are not one and the same. Neither side will be happy until you get them together.

ONE-DIMENSIONAL MAN

Do you often feel out of place when you are not working? Do you think all nonwork time is nonproductive time? This is not an unusual belief for many silent sons, and it exemplifies the problem of one-dimensional identity. Being defined by your occupation is fine when you are at work, but doesn't do much for you when you are not. If you truly define yourself by what you do, then who are you when you are not working? No matter how good we are at work, we can be painfully aware of not being as good at other things. To compensate for this, we either work more or view nonwork time as unimportant. But do we discount our children, our relationships, our interests? More importantly, are we discounting ourselves?

There is so much more to us than our occupation, but we can get stuck when it comes to accepting this and realizing our potential in other areas, especially in light of contradictory social reinforcement. We get it constantly from men and women alike. For example: Two men meet for the first time. Within thirty seconds, each asks the other, "What do you do?" Or worse: "What do you do for a *living?*" What a phrase! Does this imply work *is* life? Surely there is more to us than this.

> *My father taught me to work, but not to love it. I never did like work, and I don't deny it. I'd rather read, tell stories, crack jokes, talk, laugh, anything but work.*
> ABRAHAM LINCOLN

23

HIDDEN FEELINGS

> *Our society teaches males to think and do, but does very*
> *little to help us with our feelings. Maybe some of it just*
> *comes with age, but I think I know too many older men*
> *who are able to share few if any of their feelings.*
>
> CHRIS

How many times do you think, I'll just keep it to myself? For many silent sons, keeping our feelings and thoughts to ourselves became a way of protecting ourselves and our families from exposure to the outside world. It was also a way of trying to minimize the problems within our families by not communicating with each other. This is especially true in families that talk about everything but the dysfunction.

Keeping it inside always seems to make sense at the time. We believe it won't do any good to tell anyone anyway. Besides, we know they wouldn't understand. Our silence is rarely challenged or questioned by others. Among men there exists an unspoken expectation of silence. We can say we are having a problem, but beyond that, communication is seldom encouraged.

I once played golf with three other men. At the end of our golf game, which lasted almost five hours, we decided to get something to eat. One of the men declined, explaining that he had to go see his wife, who was in the hospital. None of us knew she was hospitalized. He never told us. We were walking, talking, and playing together for five hours and he remained totally silent about this serious situation.

Is there really a great motivation in us to keep things inside, or is it that by the time we are men we are so conditioned we aren't even aware of what we are doing? We *are* aware, however, of our pain and problems; we simply do not consider letting them out.

I suppose keeping it inside would be all right if the solutions were also inside. But usually they are not. I do believe each of us possesses within us what we need to recover, what we need to change, and what we need to become healthier men. But more often than not, we need to go outside of ourselves to understand the inside. We need to let others in to help us get to the core of ourselves, that center which holds the answers.

When you keep your pain inside, you only have one opinion and, at best, one option. When you are in pain you need alternatives, not the same old answers. Sometimes you have to leave home to find them. The pain that is inside of you is never silent. It keeps rattling around trying to find a way out. By keeping it inside you think you are keeping it quiet, but you know you still hear a hell of a lot of noise.

SHORT FUSE

Are you often angry, but don't know why? Do you get upset over "small things" very quickly? When it comes to your temper, do you have a short fuse? One of the most powerful emotions in men and silent sons is anger. But a short fuse indicates more than that. It tells you that you have *unresolved* anger inside of you. Additionally, it tells you that you possess few alternatives for dealing with stress.

Many silent sons have repressed memories of their childhoods, but the emotional impact has stayed with them and is expressed as anger.

I have often heard silent sons say, "I don't know why I explode so quickly." Maybe it's because their unresolved anger is always very close to the surface, yet they don't know it. Let's say the average man has an "anger range" from 1 to 10, with 10 representing extreme anger. On a daily basis his average anger score is a 4. Therefore, it takes an increase of 6 points to get him up to a 10. A silent son who has unresolved anger is probably walking around with an average daily score of 7 or 8 and doesn't know it, or does know it but can't identify the source. Consequently, it only takes an increase of 2 or 3 points to get him to a 10. When he gets angry so easily, he thinks it is because he has a quick temper. It seldom occurs to him that he's full of anger already.

Many men live a lifetime of silence. They don't want to admit that they are silent sons. Others hear the voices within them but do not know how to respond. Still others give voice to the silence and find great meaning in their lives. They no longer look to others to define who they are, and they no longer look to their work to provide the only meaning in their lives. What about you? What do you hear? Are you a silent son? What will you do about it? Will you wait a lifetime to acknowledge your silence, or will you allow yourself to find more in your life? Will your silence bury you or will you bury it?

Some silent sons act as if life were a rehearsal. In a rehearsal you don't give your all, because you are waiting for the real thing. Maybe this applies to your life. Do you think to yourself, In this life I'll keep quiet; in the next one I'll speak up? Are you going through the motions without emotions? What will you say when it is over? Will you say, "I did it all, I lived it all, and I said it all," or will you say, "I held back, watched a lot, never said a word, and let my life pass me by"? Much of your silence has hurt other people as much as it has hurt you.

An old man lay dying in his hospital bed. At his side was his wife of many years and his grown daughter and son. In a fading voice the old man said, "I never did enough."

His wife was the first to reply. "Don't you ever say that. You are a good husband, a good father, and a good provider."

"Yes, but I never did enough."

"Papa, don't say that—you are a wonderful man and a great father. You were always there for me. I love you Papa," said his tearful daughter.

"Yes, but I never did enough."

His son stepped forward and leaned over his father's bed. Warmly he whispered to his father, "Dad you have always been a good father. I have always looked up to you. You taught me so much."

"Yes, but I never did enough. I didn't give enough. I didn't love enough. I didn't take enough time off."

They insisted, "Papa, don't say that. You were more than we could ever ask for, you were more than enough."

"No," he said one last time. "I meant I didn't do enough for me."

AFTERTHOUGHTS

In the middle of difficulty lies opportunity.
ALBERT EINSTEIN

I was angry with my friend;
I told my wrath, my wrath did end.

I was angry with my foe;
I told it not, my wrath did grow.

WILLIAM BLAKE

It is better to wear out than to rust out.

GEORGE WHITEFIELD

This is the worst pain a man can suffer: To have insight
into much and power over nothing.

HERODOTUS

I'm exhausted from not talking.

SAM GOLDWYN

CHAPTER TWO

What Kind of Men Are We?

When someone says, "Just be yourself," what does that mean?
Who am I?

JAKE

What kind of men are we? Are we really any different from other men? Were we scarred by our past, or did we just have a difficult childhood? After all, we're doing fine now, aren't we?

I believe that to a certain degree we are different from other men. Even if we appear to be fine, even if we achieve a better life than the average man, we are still men who are hiding our pain.

I do not see us as ordinary victims. Yes, we were victimized as boys; yes, we learned many negative behaviors in order to survive. But now that we are men, we unknowingly perpetuate the problem. We have become the perpetrators—we are victims of ourselves.

What kind of men are we? Many of us are men who are all grown up and have no place to grow. We have learned to limit our emotions to such an extent that we won't let others in and we can't get out. We invest an inordinate amount of time and energy maintaining a façade, an image to hide behind.

Are you an image man? The image man upholds traditional ideas and values about men. Even when he doubts they are true, he maintains them. He is not open to alternatives which threaten his conventional image of what it means to be a male. The following are some characteristics and beliefs of the image man. Do they fit you?

- The more pain I can take, the more of a man I am.
- Showing feelings is for women.
- The more I can drink, the more manly I am.
- Intimacy is sex; sex is intimacy.
- Only women depend on others.
- A man should take care of himself without help.
- Winners never quit; quitters never win.
- No one can hurt you if you are strong.
- Men don't need friends like women do.
- I am what I do.
- I am what I earn.
- It is best to keep everything to myself.
- Men are the breadwinners.

There is an alternative to the image man—I call him the balanced man. The balanced man can explore the various dimensions of his emotional self and still feel good about being a man. He is also not easily discouraged.

It is often said that the healthiest people are androgynous—that is, they possess the best aspects of being male and female. Each of us possesses the ability not only to identify with the other gender but also to share each other's qualities. This does not mean that you have to slight your masculinity or femininity to "make room" for the androgynous side of yourself. In fact, you actually *add* to yourself. You can further develop and enhance all of your qualities and become more of a man. The balanced man wants to know more about himself, his world, and how to better himself. The image man is like the cartoon character Popeye, when he says, "I am who I am and that's all I am." The balanced man says, "I know who I am and what I could be." Some characteristics of a balanced man are:

- He's not ashamed to ask for help.
- He says "I'm sorry" when he's wrong.

- He feels good about himself.
- He has a sense of worth separate from his job.
- He knows how to appropriately handle anger.
- He can correctly identify his feelings.
- He is flexible in a crisis.
- He has a healthy sense of humor.
- He asks directions.
- He is a good listener.
- He does not feel threatened by his own feelings.

If you identify only with the characteristics of the image man, you aren't open to any "healthy alternatives." You need to wrestle with what you have been taught; you need to fight against your image of yourself. It's not going to be easy, but it can be done.

> *The freedom I feel today may not be complete, but it is far better, far more serene than anything I have ever known before. Don't be afraid of your feelings. Real men do feel. Real men do cry, are vulnerable, and trusting. Your real feelings won't kill you. Stuffing them will.*
>
> JOHN

Robert Fisher in his book, *The Knight in Rusty Armor,* talks about a knight in shining armor who spends all of his time polishing that armor, along with his image.[1] The knight spends so much time doing this that those around him, including his family, don't know him anymore—he never spends any time with them, and eventually they want to leave. He then decides he is willing to change, to give up his armor. But he discovers that he has been in the armor for so long that the seams have rusted together—he *can't* get out.

The knight thought the armor would protect him, but it only kept others out and him a prisoner. It may have made him look strong, but in fact it weakened him. He was betrayed by the very guise he worked so hard to uphold.

The image man spends a lot of time, money, and energy polishing his armor. The balanced man knows *he* is his armor.

Gregory, 42, was recently divorced. His father was a compulsive gambler and womanizer. As a boy Gregory thought his father was a "real man." He tried to imitate his father and live up to his image of what a man was. Today Gregory feels betrayed by what he was taught. He has lost his wife and children. He doesn't know if he can accept help, because it makes him uncomfortable, but he does want to change. He states, "I see so many mind games—you know, playing out scenarios in our minds. And in our minds we do what Charles Bronson or John Wayne would do."

We are all products of our culture, but some of us are prisoners of it. It is not easy to shed an image when it is reinforced every day by other men and women.

Our culture is slowly accepting alternative male images, but the traditional stereotype still dominates. We are constantly bombarded by messages reinforcing the social expectations of what a man *should* be and think:

- Be rational; be logical.
- Business before pleasure.
- There's no such thing as too much money.
- Winning isn't everything—it's the only thing.
- A husband's job is to be a good provider.
- Never let them see you sweat.
- Drink like a man.
- Real men don't _____.

Sometimes it is difficult for us to see the influence of social expectations on our daily behaviors. Ask yourself the following questions to see how you have been influenced by society and how much you influence others:[2]

- Do your obligations to work usually take precedence over your family?
- Does your wife/partner complain about your need for sex and how closed off you seem?
- Do friends remark that they never can predict when you will open up with them about personal issues?
- Are you so difficult to get along with that you don't have any really close male friends?
- Are you getting tired of always being "on the go"?

31

- Are you always clear about how you think and seldom aware of how you feel?
- Can you stay in a disagreeable conversation with friends without getting mad, giving up, changing the subject, or finding an exit before there is some closure?
- Exactly how many minutes of relaxed, caring time did you spend with your children today, yesterday, last week, last year?

DIFFERENCES AMONG SILENT SONS

Despite similar cultural or social influences, not all silent sons are the same. One-size-fits-all doesn't apply to those of us from troubled families. While it is true that we share some similarities, we are largely dissimilar. In fact, I have met many silent sons whose brothers were not silent sons. There are at least seven reasons why we are not all affected in the same ways: the degree of your parent's (or parents') dysfunction, the type and kind of parents you had, your stress level, your age, your perception of the situation, cultural influences, and offsetting factors.

DEGREE OF DYSFUNCTION IN YOUR PARENT(S)

"Degree of dysfunction" refers to how significantly your parent's dysfunction affected his or her parenting ability. Likewise, it concerns how much your dysfunctional parent affected your non-dysfunctional (or less dysfunctional) parent's ability to fulfill his or her role as a mother or father.

Silent sons whose parents were dysfunctional but still able to perform some parental duties did not suffer the same scarring as those with alcoholic parents who were seldom sober or parents who left the family for extended periods of time. Families are dysfunctional by degree, not by absolutes. When some silent sons confess, "It wasn't so bad," they may mean that their parents were nurturing at least some of the time.

TYPE AND KIND OF DYSFUNCTIONAL PARENT

The type of dysfunctional parent or parents you had can effect different outcomes. "Type of parent" refers to personality type, while "kind of parent" refers to the specific kinds of dysfunctional behaviors that you endured. For example, having a father with a moody personality who exhibits violent behavior can be a lot different from having a mother with a dependent personality who suffers from depression.

I found that the personality of the parent or parents played a large role in how sons perceived the extent of their family's problems. For example, there were silent sons who were angry with their fathers and had a low opinion of them because the fathers were simply difficult to be around. Behavior and personality are not the same. However, many silent sons were not sure which was worse—their parents' dysfunctional behavior or their parents' personality, such as obsessive-compulsive, overly demanding, or extremely rigid character.

STRESS

Families under stress produce children under stress. Children under stress who do not receive help become adults under stress. Have you found yourself under stress, not handling it well, and asking yourself, What's happening to me, what's wrong with me? Stress can bring out your unresolved issues. Like many silent sons, you may be at a low boiling point but not realize it. When stress occurs, your reactions are extreme and you don't understand why.

Perhaps your problems are more likely to surface in particular stressful situations, while you handle other situations well. Or, are you one of the silent sons who comes alive under stress? You are used to stress—it doesn't make you uncomfortable. However, when no stress is present, you don't know what to do or how to react in normal situations.

You may have never learned how to live with stress; rather, you learned stressful ways of living. You reacted by treating everything as if it were a crisis or as if you had to be in charge. How does this affect you today?

Many silent sons, even though they want their family life to be different, find that being around their own families is very difficult for them. Family life demands emotional closeness. For many silent sons emotional closeness is stressful, even if they want it more than anything else.

AGE

How old were you when the dysfunction began in your family? There is a big difference between silent sons who were born into a dysfunctional family and those whose family became dysfunctional when they were 15.

How long you were exposed to the dysfunction is another factor. The general rule is, the longer you were exposed, the higher the probability of negative effects.

If the dysfunction stopped, how old were you? A son who has a recovering alcoholic mother may have an entirely different attitude than one whose mother is still drinking or died drinking.

Finally, how old are you now? I found that most silent sons experienced problems in their thirties. But I believe that this is not just an age factor but also a stress factor. During our thirties we are dealing with relationships, parenting, career decisions, financial responsibilities, and the first indications that we are not immortal.

Age also reveals that not all problems silent sons face are due solely to their backgrounds. Some of our problems are the result of our being men at a certain age. What is bothering you now that you weren't aware of ten years ago? There are many differences between silent sons in their twenties and those in their forties, simply due to age.

PERCEPTION

One of the greatest differences I find among silent sons is their perceptions of what happened to them. Perception is truly an individual phenomenon. Even among brothers it is not the same. I once sat in a support group with two young men who were twins. They were in their early twenties, college students living at home. Both of their parents were alcoholic and extremely dysfunctional. Barry complained about his parents weekly, voicing concerns about how he dealt with them, and how he could keep doing everything that needed to be done. His brother, Michael, rarely said a word, but seemed rather amused by Barry and appeared calm most of the time. It was obvious that he had a totally different perception of the problem and his role in his parents' situation. Once Barry accused Michael, "And you, you just go about your business doing whatever you like. How can you do that?" Michael calmly replied that his parents were going to drink no matter what he did and that he was going to live his life the way he wanted. Michael seemed neither defensive nor in denial about what was happening with his parents or his brother. He simply had a different perception of the family's problems and himself.

CULTURAL CONSIDERATIONS

Our religion, race, ethnicity, and socioeconomic status greatly impact our reactions to dysfunction in our families. For example, I discovered that black silent sons scored lower in measurements of the negative effects of dysfunctional families but were affected more by societal pressures. Native American silent sons focused almost exclusively on their families in their interviews. Test showed that Hispanic silent sons require the highest levels of affirmation and approval from others, a need to control other people, an unwillingness to use alternatives, and low self-esteem. They were also the most likely to admit that violence occurred in their families. White silent sons were more likely to see their issues on an individual level and less as a reflection on their family.

Though we are all part of our culture, it does affect us differently, whether by limiting our opportunities in life or affecting the degree to which we and our families are socially accepted by others. For example, childhood would be different for the son of a white Irish Catholic father who drinks too much than for the son of a black Southern Baptist father who drinks too much.

Whether or not you are aware of cultural considerations, you may find yourself explaining to an outsider, "We just don't do that in my family," or "You have to understand how we are." When you make these statements, you are taking into account that you are product of your environment. Your culture can work for or against you. I have spoken with silent sons who fear prejudice and other unfair cultural standards as much as they fear the dysfunction in their own families. I have also heard silent sons talk about how their extended family or community made a positive difference in their lives.

OFFSETTING FACTORS

Sometimes a person or an institution can have a positive impact on your childhood and thus help to offset the negativity of a dysfunctional family. Did any one person or organization do this for you? Was there one special friend or relative who made a marked difference in your life?

Two very powerful offsetting factors in my life were my paternal grandmother and school. My grandmother always asked me about my father's drinking when we were alone. I knew she understood what was happening in our family, and it was comforting not to feel alone. We never solved the problems, but she kept me from feeling completely isolated and helpless.

School helped me a lot also. I felt like I was my own person in school and not just a member of "that family." School was a place where I could feel good about myself. It was an emotional oasis and I liked being there. My grades weren't great, but my self-esteem was better.

COMMON ISSUES

As silent sons we share many common issues, but some of us never overcame the trouble as boys and are still having problems as men— either in our relationships or in our careers or with addiction or antisocial behavior. Others do all right on the surface, but are troubled inside and don't know why. Still others know themselves very well, can roll with the punches, and always land on their feet. Regardless of which of these patterns apply, I have observed an unspoken comradeship between silent sons. Maybe we don't know what it is, but we do share something about our pasts with each other.

Let's look at some of the common behaviors of silent sons and you can see how you compare to other silent sons and also to men from functional families.

Below you will find a number of statements indicative of different personality characteristics grouped into seven dimensions of behavior. Rank each statement using the following scale and add up your score:

5 = always
4 = often
3 = sometimes
2 = seldom
1 = never

Perceived Isolation

_____ I guess at what is normal.
_____ I feel different from other people.
_____ I have difficulty with intimate relationships.

Inconsistency

_____ I have difficulty following projects through to the end.
_____ I look for immediate as opposed to deferred gratification.
_____ I manage my time poorly and do not set my priorities in a way that works well for me.

Self-Condemnation

_____ I judge myself without mercy.
_____ I have difficulty having fun.
_____ I take myself very seriously.

Control Needs

_____ I overreact to changes over which I have no control.
_____ I am either super-responsible or irresponsible.

Approval Needs

_____ I constantly seek approval and affirmation.

_____ I am extremely loyal even in the face of evidence that the loyalty is undeserved.

_____ I lie when it would be just as easy to tell the truth.

Rigidity

_____ I lock myself into a course of action without serious consideration to alternate choices or consequences.

_____ I seek tension and crisis and then complain.

_____ I avoid conflict or aggravate it, but rarely deal with it.

Fear of Failure

_____ I fear rejection and abandonment, yet I reject others.

_____ I fear failure, but I downgrade my successes.

_____ I fear criticism and judgment, yet I criticize others.

If you scored 50 or lower, you show a below-average identification with the problems associated with being raised in a dysfunctional family. A score of 51 to 70 indicates an average impact, and a score above 71 indicates an above-average response. Obviously, the higher your score, the more negatively you were affected by the dysfunctional family experience. Of course, your score depends also upon your level of awareness of your behaviors and your degree of denial about them.

The differences between silent sons and men from functional families are interesting (see Tables 4 and 5 Appendix). In most cases—eighteen out of twenty of the above characteristics—silent sons scored higher, indicating not only that they were affected by their dysfunctional families, but also that the effects were widespread and consistent. The highest average score for a personality characteristic for silent sons was for "I take myself very seriously."

The two highest combined measurements for silent sons were in perceived isolation and fear of failure. This is not surprising. We all feel lonely at times and have fears about failing, but the degree of concern is much higher for silent sons than for men raised in functional families.

It's hard to share when you think of yourself as the only one in the world.

JEROME

MEN AND CO-DEPENDENCY: FACT, FICTION, OR FAD?

One of the most common statements heard about people who were raised in dysfunctional families is that they are likely to develop co-dependency. What is co-dependency? "Co-dependency" is a term coined to describe a condition that develops in people as a result of living with a chemically dependent person. However, it is now applied to other dysfunctional situations.

Of all the definitions of co-dependency, the one that I like best is by Robert Subby, a psychologist and author of *Lost in the Shuffle*. He defines co-dependency as: "an emotional, psychological, and behavioral condition that develops as a result of an individual's prolonged exposure to, and practice of, a set of oppressive rules—rules which prevent the open expression of feeling, as well as the direct discussion of personal and interpersonal problems."[3]

Glover, age 52, is a prototype of a man who grew up restrained by oppressive rules. His father owned an auto repair business. He was an alcoholic who was verbally abusive and extremely rigid in his opinions. Everyone in Glover's family feared his father. As a boy, Glover would try to please his father in order to keep him from getting upset and drinking. As a result, Glover overly identified with his father's need not to get upset and seldom did anything about his own needs. In fact, he learned never to ask for what he wanted or to express his opinions or emotions at home. Today Glover is having problems in his own family. He tries to please everyone in his family and meet all their needs. When they aren't "happy" he gets upset. He cannot tolerate differences in opinion, has difficulty getting close to his children and wife, and is becoming more withdrawn. Glover wants to change, but is still following his father's rules. The core of his problem is that he still fails to express his emotions and needs. Although he no longer lives under his father's roof, Glover is still a prisoner.

Co-dependency is not about victimization as much as it is about lost opportunity. Co-dependency for men is a condition that can keep us from reaching our potential emotionally, psychologically, spiritually, and behaviorally. Have you ever felt that you are not really yourself in many situations because you are holding something back? Have you been told by your partner that he or she never quite knows you because you always hold something back? Do you find yourself not taking the risks you need to at work because you are holding back? Co-dependency limits you.

Women feel more comfortable talking about co-dependency than men because it has been applied to many of their behaviors. Even though discussions of co-dependency can often be seen as "blaming the victim," most women seem not to resent the label and actively seek help with the problem. Men, however, are not as comfortable with admitting co-dependency because we are unsure of what it is, how it applies to us, and whether or not we can be co-dependent and still be masculine.

Co-dependency is also influenced by social expectations for men and women. For women, the qualities associated with being a woman and the qualities associated with being co-dependent are often one and the same. For example, the problems some women have with power, control, equality, self-esteem, exploitation, and overidentification with the needs of others are often the same as those associated with co-dependency. Therefore, when women admit to being co-dependent, they seldom challenge their gender identity. My experience has actually shown that many women from dysfunctional families begin to talk about their co-dependency before they talk about their issues of being a woman.[4]

Men do the opposite. If a man is willing to talk about himself, and he is a silent son, he will want to begin by talking about men's issues before he'd ever talk about his dysfunctional background. He is more likely to attend workshops on being male, such as those conducted by Robert Bly, Sam Keen, or John Lee, before he'll move on to other issues. A man wants to feel like a man before he feels anything else.

As men we may have ignored the problem of co-dependency because it has challenged our manhood. Such a challenge is never taken lightly. We will fight before we accept something we don't understand.

If you are a silent son and are having problems today, ask yourself: Do you really understand what is happening to you? Do you know what you are fighting, or do you just know you are at war?

It is possible that men are not quite as affected by a dysfunctional family as women. Or maybe it just affects men differently. I asked a group of counselors to list how they saw co-dependency manifested in men. These are some of their responses:

- The man overly depends on women to act out his emotional side.
- He controls situations to extremes; he must always do it *his* way.
- He is a workaholic.
- He is good at rescuing and protecting, but not interacting.
- If a father, he may be living through his son.
- He exhibits stress disorders.
- His relationships are filled with anger.
- He uses other males for ego strength.
- He has a problem with addiction.
- He lacks emotional expression.
- He has one dimension of self-worth—his occupation.
- He has a fear of intimacy.
- He lacks spirituality.
- He is externally validated only by what he does.
- He exhibits extreme rigidity.
- He overly asserts his masculinity.

Women who are co-dependent may overidentify with being feminine and disproportionately nurture others to meet their needs. Men who are co-dependent overidentify with being masculine and carry this identity to an extreme, which results in the loss of their identity. The silent son who is co-dependent has an underdeveloped sense of self. To find out who he is, he must constantly turn outward to others. Co-dependency keeps the silent son trapped. You can become trapped by thinking that you must always be in control, must always protect everyone, must never show emotion, must always pretend you know what you are doing, or must always be loyal to the image. The man who is trapped cannot find his way out, because he only knows the ways of others; he has none of his own. A man who is trapped is a man in pain. He is a man denying his potential. I believe what keeps us trapped more than anything else is upholding the stereotypical image of being male. The stronger the allegiance to this image, the more powerful co-dependency can become. Co-dependency means you are someone else's man. Freedom means you are your own.

Does overcoming co-dependency mean you must be less of a man? Absolutely not. It actually means becoming more of a man. It means having the courage to get beyond your own dysfunctional problems *and* beyond the societal, stereotypical image of what it means to be a man.

During the past fifteen years I have been involved with my own growth and that of many men throughout this country. At no time did I feel my masculinity was being challenged. I did feel challenged on a personal level—challenged to open up, to break down emotional barriers, to surmount unnecessary limitations, to get on with my life. Some of the healthiest men I know and some of my most respected mentors have been men who have struggled with much trouble in their lives and won the battles. These men did not fear the label of co-dependency or any other condition. What they feared most was what would happen to them if they did not embrace change. All of these men overcame their limitations. And they never stopped being men.

AFTERTHOUGHTS

> *Most people are about as happy as they make up their minds to be.*
>
> ABRAHAM LINCOLN

> *Honesty is the first chapter in the book of wisdom.*
>
> THOMAS JEFFERSON

> *A diamond is a chunk of coal that made good under pressure.*
>
> ANONYMOUS

The chains of habit are too weak to be felt until they are too strong to be broken.

SAMUEL JOHNSON

Be a philosopher, but amid all your philosophy be still a man.

DAVID HUME

CHAPTER THREE

Where Do You Stand?

Are you aware of how what you learned in childhood affects you today? Are you aware that you have developed interaction patterns—both with your inner self and with people around you—that you use over and over again regardless of whether they have positive or negative consequences? How well do you know your own personality? Can you write a list of your positive as well as any negative characteristics as a result of growing up in a dysfunctional family?

TYPES OF SILENT SONS

I have observed enough differences in silent sons to isolate eight different types. Each of these types has positive as well as negative characteristics. Traditionally, when most therapists, counselors, and others talk about adults from dysfunctional families they tend to focus on the negative. It amazes me that that's all they can see. Silent sons are survivors, and it takes strength and skill to survive. Many of these skills are, or can become, positive characteristics. Additionally, since we are affected by degree, it only makes sense that some silent sons have more positive or negative characteristics than others.

These types I enumerate below are not mutually exclusive. Some overlap. For example, you might find that you identify very strongly with one of the types, but that you also have some of the characteristics of two others.

I have arranged the types according to how strongly each identifies with the male stereotype image, dividing them into strong, moderate, and low. As discussed in the previous chapter, it appears that both men and women who suffer from co-dependency have an extremely loyal relationship with their stereotypical gender image. The stronger the stereotype, the more difficult it is to break co-dependent patterns. For example, the silent son with a highly stereotypical male image is likely to be very rigid, deny most of his emotions, have difficulty getting close to others, and is not likely to try alternatives. He basically knows only one way to deal with himself and with the world. The less the silent son identifies with the stereotype, the more open he is to alternatives and the less he is locked into rigid patterns. He too, can have problems, but he will fit into a different type than the high-image male.

Your male image has been developing over a long time. You have probably been working on it since childhood. It will not be easy to break, because it has become like a "habit cage." It keeps you locked in and others locked out. Don't be surprised to find that some of the characteristics you once considered positive are now negative. It is very likely that what you did to survive as a boy can hold you back as an adult. For example, if your parents' home was extremely chaotic, one of the ways you were able to reduce the stress was to take control of as much of your environment as possible. This might have worked in times of chaos, but in normal times feeling you must always be in charge works against you and alienates others. In order to change our negative patterns we need to make transitions, which involves giving up old behaviors and adopting new ones, in order to develop our positive characteristics. Indicated at the end of each typology are some of the transitions necessary for us to make these changes.

STRONG IDENTIFICATION WITH MALE IMAGE

Silent sons with a highly stereotypical image of being male are usually very competitive, courageous, distant, and silent; they don't show pain and they do follow the "macho" man credo. Unfortunately, they are also very angry silent sons, and their rigidity makes it difficult for them to break these patterns. The following types apply.

THE TRIANGULATOR

The triangulator is the silent son who never learned to deal with anything directly. When there are problems, he always wants to find some external focus on which to place the blame. Usually he learned this pattern as a boy when he became the external focus for the problems between his parents. As soon as he started acting out, the parents not only focused exclusively on him as the problem in the family, but also blamed him as the source of the family's problems. The fact that his mother was an alcoholic or his father was abusive was not seen as the problem by them. In their minds, it was their son who was the problem.

The triangulator has difficulty accepting responsibility for his behavior. Besides, he thinks it's always the other guy's fault. He is angry at the world, and he resents how he is being treated.

If you are a triangulator, do you often hear from your partner that you don't know how to communicate, and do you usually respond to this by getting angry? Is it difficult for you to see that you are equally responsible for the success of a relationship? Do you find it difficult to get close to someone because no one understands you?

The triangulator *thinks* he is extremely independent, but in fact he is very dependent on everyone—not only to tolerate his behavior but also to provide a place for his blame. His inappropriate image of a male makes it difficult for him to think that there is anything wrong with his anger; it is always "them," not him.

The positive and negative characteristics of the triangulator are:

Positive

He is creative.
He is courageous.
He is good under pressure.
He has lots of friends.
He commands attention.
He is adventuresome.

Negative

He exhibits conduct disorders.

He has poor communication skills.

He blames the world for his problems.

He is manipulative.

He is angry.

He is irresponsible.

He presents a high risk for addiction.

He has an antisocial personality.

He is passive-aggressive.

Transitions Needed

· Learn to accept responsibility for your behaviors.

· Learn appropriate ways to handle or release anger.

· Learn how to communicate directly.

· Learn alternative ways to handle stress.

THE DETACHER

When you were about 15, did you try to detach yourself from what was happening in your family by telling yourself, "It doesn't bother me"? Did you think the solution to everything at home was to stay out of the house as much as possible? Were you counting the days until you could move out? If so, you probably learned detaching behaviors. Not all detachment is negative. Knowing when to detach yourself from an unhealthy situation can be healthy, but the kind of detachment that is negative is called "premature closure." This occurs when you detach yourself from a situation at the first sign of trouble. You leave even before you see whether or not the problem can be worked out. When this happens you never learn conflict resolution, you only learn how to leave.

Do you find yourself saying that your childhood didn't bother you, that what your father or mother did doesn't bother you—just don't bring it up? The detacher thinks that because he has physically detached he has also emotionally detached. This is rarely the case. The silent son detacher fears exposing his pain and his vulnerability. He is afraid of getting hurt.

The detacher is likely to go through many unsuccessful relationships. No relationship is trouble free, but at the first sign of trouble the detacher's tapes start playing "It's time to leave." For example, a detacher silent son might go through relationships with eight women. All of the relationships collapse and all for the same reason. What does he conclude? That all women have problems, or that they all have the same problem and the only way to handle them is leave. The detacher is afraid to get involved. He treats every relationship like a boxing match: Protect yourself at all times. He seldom realizes he is getting hit with his own punches. Maybe his detachment protects him, but it also makes him lonely.

The positive and negative characteristics of the detacher silent son are:

Positive

He is perceptive.
He sets limits.
He can spot trouble.
He is independent.
He is self-motivated.
He is a good traveler.

Negative

He has rigid attitudes.
He is jealous, suspicious.
He is defiant.
He is lonely.
He is insensitive to his feelings.
He poses a high risk for addiction.
He is secretive.
He holds inner anger.
He fears being hurt.
He frequently resorts to denial of problems.

Transitions Needed

- Learn interpersonal relationship skills.
- Develop a realistic concept of a healthy relationship.
- Develop alternatives for handling stress.
- Learn to identify and express your emotions.
- Learn to accept help and support from others.

MODERATE IDENTIFICATION WITH MALE IMAGE

The silent son with a moderate degree of identification with the stereotypical male image has the problems of an average male, compounded by a dysfunctional family background. Thus he experiences the average problems to a greater degree. Like other men he is worried about his job, but he is more likely to become a workaholic. Like other men he wants to be a good father, but he finds it hard to be close to his family and make time for them. Like other men he has relationship problems, but old habits keep coming up and complicating his relationships. He is not, however, as rigid as the strong-identification-image silent son, and therefore has a greater capacity for alternatives. He is often liked and admired by others, but hides a low self-esteem. He is a man of mixed feelings not only about his past, but also about himself. He is trying to find balance in his life, but feels pulled in many directions. There are two types of silent sons who fit the moderate-identification-image male. These are the achiever and the hyper-mature.

THE ACHIEVER

Are you the most competent guy you know? Are you the most competent guy others have ever met? Are you so organized that you make the bed when you get up in the middle of the night to go to the bathroom? Do you also have an empty feeling inside of you that you are never good enough and that you are only as good as your accomplishments that others can see? If so, welcome to the achievers' club.

Don't get me wrong; there is nothing wrong with achievement. But there is more to life.

The achiever pattern is very difficult to break for men because it is so much a part of our culture. We simply believe we are what we do, and we are nothing if we haven't done anything.

The achiever pattern develops very early for the silent son. It was often through his achievements and only his achievements that he got any recognition in his family. Therefore, if he wanted attention, which he equated with approval, he had better perform.

Many men who fall into this pattern become workaholics. They are driven by external forces, such as the need for validation, which unfortunately they believe only comes from others. They seldom have an internal sense of self-worth and they feel inadequate most of the time, even when they do something well. Nothing is ever enough for them. It might be enough for others, but not for them.

Many achievers are perfectionists. Being a perfectionist is bad enough, but it is much worse when an achiever projects onto other people or other things. For example, most achievers spend most of their lives being disappointed. Nothing ever lives up to their expectations. They have such high ideals about people and things that no one or no thing can match them. It seldom occurs to achievers that their ideals are not realistic. They often find themselves asking why others can't do what they are supposed to do.

If you are an achiever, you are probably very good at taking care of others. But do you sacrifice yourself in order to achieve some goal? And do you find that having reached one goal, you immediately set the next?

There's nothing wrong with having goals, but the achiever reaches his and never takes time to enjoy his accomplishments. Maybe that's because he never thinks anything he does is good enough, and he never thinks he is good enough either. Stopping to smell the roses is not one of his goals, because it makes him reflect on what's really important in his life. The achiever talks a good game about what's important, but he seldom takes time for these things. He says he values his family, but he doesn't value his time with them. Maybe he thinks time spent with his family is nonproductive time.

The achiever is usually in an internal struggle. He struggles against what he believes and what he thinks he must do to make himself feel good. The trick in our lives is to get the two together. An internal sense of worth is just as important to the healthy man as an external sense of worth. However, it takes a healthy man to realize this.

In relationships the achiever is often accused by his partner of being more of a parent than a lover. His need to be in charge subtly dominates the relationship, but at the same time he is usually dependent on his partner to nurture the emotional side of the relationship. He needs it, but can't give it. In relationships the achiever is the classic intellectualizer, because of an inability to express his feelings, but he looks good and does all the right behavioral things. He just isn't "in" the relationship. It is ironic that like many silent sons he feels something is missing in his relationships, which is usually what his partner is saying too. It is not uncommon for the achiever to be looking for more and more in a relationship, which often means he looks outside his current one.

These are the positive and negative characteristics of the achiever:

Positive

He is competent.
He is good in a crisis.
He is reliable.
He meets goals.
He takes charge well.
He is successful.
He is a survivor.
He motivates self and others.

Negative

He is overly competitive.
He is a perfectionist.
He has difficulty relaxing.
He fails to take care of himself.
He can't express feelings.
He needs external validation.

51

He is a workaholic.
He is never wrong.
He marries a dependent person.
He exhibits compulsive behavior.
He disproportionately fears failure.
He is unable to play.

Transitions Needed

- Develop an *internal* sense of validation in yourself.
- Learn to say no to others and yourself.
- Find time for yourself.
- Learn to relax, slow down.
- Learn to appreciate yourself.

THE HYPERMATURE

Closely associated with the achiever is the hypermature silent son. However, whereas the achiever's problems are evident in his behavior, the hypermature betrays himself with his attitude. The hypermature silent son is too serious all the time. He is emotionally on guard at all times. He never lets his defenses down or lets himself go. Maintaining control in his life is an understatement. To him, "Be prepared" is not the Boy Scout motto, it's a way of life and the *only* way he knows to live. Author and British philosopher G. K. Chesterton tells us that the reason that angels can fly is because they take themselves lightly. This type of guy will never get off the ground. He fears exposure and loss of control.

If you are a hypermature silent son, chances are you are far too self-critical, have difficulty having fun, and live under a high level of stress. Taking risks is not exactly your daily routine.

Hypermaturity comes from having too many responsibilities as a child and never having time for normal childhood activities. The hypermature silent son never had time to play. Life was too serious and a sense of humor had no purpose for him. It was a tough way to grow up and now he only knows how to be tough, especially on himself.

In relationships the hypermature silent son is intense. It is difficult for him to take things easy. He is often analytical and feels responsible for the success of a relationship. He can spend more time trying to make the relationship "work" than enjoying it. Fun is missing in his relationships, and as a result, too often so is his partner. The hypermature man wants laughter, warmth, and closeness, but doesn't know how to achieve them and has difficulty letting himself go long enough to try. Change is slow for him, and he needs a patient partner who can see a great person behind the seriousness. Besides, he will never let you down.

The positive and negative personality characteristics of the hypermature silent son are:

Positive

He is organized.
He is analytical.
He is prepared.
He is mature.
He is reliable.
He is intuitive.
He meets goals.
He is attentive.

Negative

He is too serious.
He has difficulty expressing emotions.
He constantly needs to be in control.
He may exhibit stress-related illnesses.
He doesn't have much fun.
He is fearful.
He is driven.
He avoids taking risks.
He is critical.
He blames himself too much.

53

Transitions Needed

- Learn to relax and have fun.
- Learn to let others take charge.
- Learn to allow yourself to express emotions.
- Learn to adjust priorities to reduce feeling overwhelmed.
- Laugh more.

LOW IDENTIFICATION WITH MALE IMAGE

Are you usually more concerned about another's feelings than your own? Do you find yourself always going out of your way to help other people, even if you don't want to? Do you wish that you could say no to people? Are you overly concerned with what people will think about you? If so, you may be have a low degree of identification with the male image.

As a result of your past experiences, you may be more likely than other men to fear rejection and thus are more willing to take on the problems and concerns of others as a way of feeling needed. You may also be concerned about whether you are masculine enough. You don't jump right into many of the things that other men do or take for granted. Your concerns are usually a combination of masculinity and your dysfunctional background. There are three types of silent sons having low identification with male image.

THE PASSIVE SON

> *I had many conflicts, particularly in adolescence, with my father, always verbal. I always lost or was put down. This undermined my self-confidence in my mental abilities. Although I have above-average intelligence and a master's degree, I am extremely cautious about expressing my own opinions even when I have strong ones. Also, I have a lot of trouble being creative.*
>
> CHESTER

The passive silent son acts as if life is a spectator sport. He has difficulty getting into the game. He is content to sit on the sidelines and watch, but secretly wishes he was playing, yet he doesn't feel comfortable getting involved. Unlike many of the other types who exhibit some particular behaviors, the passive type is very difficult to break out of because of what the man is *not* doing. When it comes to his own interest and issues he doesn't take a stand. He feels relatively unimportant compared to other people, and doesn't believe he has much to offer. As a boy this was the message he received from his parents. Eventually he began to believe it, and as a man he is living it.

In relationships, he puts his needs second. He is likely to tolerate a tremendous amount of inappropriate behavior from a partner. He doesn't stick up for himself and as a result feels stuck. He believes he has few options. He is at high risk of being used and then abandoned in favor of a more interesting partner. He is left scratching his head and asking, "But what did I do?" Nothing, absolutely nothing. To change, the passive silent son does not need to break old behaviors so much as he needs to develop new ones. Passivity is not changed by inaction.

The positive and negative characteristics of the passive silent son are:

Positive

He is tolerant.
He is willing to help others.
He is highly adaptable.
He is a loyal friend.
He is independent.
He is a good listener.
He is empathic.

Negative

He doesn't stand up for himself.
He has low self-worth.

He always puts others first.
He is lonely.
He fears reality.
He is depressed.
He lacks joy.
He is often used in relationships.
He is overly shy.
He is unsure of his male identity.

Transitions Needed

- Learn to take care of yourself first.
- Do things to raise your self-esteem.
- Learn to feel good about yourself.
- Learn to accept being liked by others.
- Stop doing nothing; take action.

THE CONFLICT AVOIDER

Will you do anything to avoid a conflict? Or will you do anything to keep from truly resolving it? In an argument, is your goal to stop it or to resolve it?

Silent sons who are conflict avoiders can fool you. On the surface they appear to be extremely competent with helping others with their problems. They are usually the guys everyone goes to with their problems. After all, they have been raised in crisis situations and are very good at telling others how to handle them. However, the conflict avoiders are rarely able to handle their own crises. The more they help others, the easier it is to keep people away from *their* issues. The greatest problem for conflict avoiders is their inability to receive from others. They simply cannot allow themselves to be emotionally supported or helped by other people. They can give closeness, but not receive it.

> *I find myself living defensively. I also find that I withhold a piece of myself. If I don't allow myself to get too close to you, I can't get hurt when you leave.*
>
> MORRIS

As a boy, the conflict avoider saw many arguments, but never any resolution. This left him with the wrong idea not only about arguments, but also about relationships. He thought that there was no such thing as a healthy argument. He learned that he hated conflict, so he became the peacemaker. Reconciling conflicting parties—or keeping the peace—became a useful thing for him to do. Helping others is certainly admirable, but you can also take on too many problems, internalize them, and become depressed yourself.

In relationships, the conflict avoider is at a high risk of becoming involved with a needy person. He thinks that because he is needed he is important to the other person. He is also at a high risk of being used. He fears rejection and will do anything to keep conflict out of his relationships. He pretends there are no problems and believes it is his responsibility to take care of them when they do occur.

The greatest problem for this silent son is his own internal conflict. He is not about to acknowledge it and consistently tells himself he is not angry. Nothing is resolved. He tries to pretend his conflict does not exist by preoccupying himself with everyone else's problems, but it doesn't work. In the end, the conflict avoider is avoiding himself. His own problems are his greatest fear.

The positive and negative personality characteristics of the silent son conflict avoider are:

Positive

He is willing to help others.
He is good in a crisis.
He is a good negotiator.
He is a problem solver.
He is persistent.
He is sensitive to others.
He thinks of alternatives.
He is a good communicator.

Negative

He has an unrealistic view of arguments.
He is constantly placating others.
He feels powerless.
He suffers from depression.
He is in denial.
He takes on too many problems.
He is seldom happy.
He is easily intimidated.
He lacks the ability to receive support from others.
He is used in relationships.

Transitions Needed

- Recognize and focus on your own problems.
- Quit taking on the problems of others.
- Learn to accept positive attention.
- Learn the difference between helping someone and feeling responsible for their problems and solutions.
- Be willing to receive help from others.

THE OTHER-DIRECTED ONE

As a boy, the other-directed silent son learned to display the exact opposite of how he felt. Often he would do this by making jokes about everything. His only way to handle pain is to treat it as if it doesn't exist. He is afraid that if he stops laughing he will cry, or worse, he will have to admit that he has been affected by the problems in his life. There are also other ways to become other-directed; some men exhibiting this pattern constantly do only what others think they should do in order to avoid rejection or being put down.

> *I could never please my father. Now I find myself instinc-*
> *tively looking for pats on the back. Did I do good?*
>
> BART

The other-directed silent son does not have a clear vision of reality. To protect himself he looks at reality through other people's eyes. He even sees himself strictly as he thinks others see him. He has no sense of self and is therefore easily influenced by others. He always has to check with someone else before he can make up his mind. He fears having his needs exposed, being abandoned by others, and being hurt. He believes that to be accepted by others he must do what they want and only what they want. He becomes a people pleaser and neglects taking care of himself.

In relationships, the other-directed silent son is always on "date behavior." Remember date behavior? You were so charming and well-mannered, especially on your first couple of dates. You wanted to be what you thought the other person wanted you to be. You were even willing to go to movies you couldn't stand in order not to offend. Eventually, perhaps a healthy relationship did emerge, one where you could be yourself and your partner still wanted to be around you. However, the other-directed silent son is still and always will be on date behavior, unless he can change. Eventually these patterns will work against him because his partner always feels that he or she can't really get to know him.

Joking around is fine to break the ice, and a partner often enjoys the funny-guy stuff for a while. But if a silent son can't let another person in, the enjoyment disappears.

The positive and negative personality characteristics of the other-directed silent son are:

Positive

He easily attracts attention.
He is charming.
He has a sense of humor.
He can anticipate the needs of others.
He is adaptable.
He is a team player.
He is cooperative.
He can appear joyful.
He is energetic.

Negative

He is overly controlled by others.
He is tense, anxious.
He overreacts.
His relationships are shallow.
He is indecisive.
He has no sense of self.
He is overly dependent.
He needs to please others.
He needs constant approval.
He has a poor sense of boundaries.

Transitions Needed

• Learn to develop a sense of what is right for you.
• Stop being controlled by others.
• Learn to express your needs and ideas.
• Establish your own sense of self and boundaries.
• Start doing what you want to do.

THE HEALTHY SURVIVOR

The healthy survivor is different than the previous seven types. He does not fit into any one of the stereotype image patterns. He is his own man, he knows what he wants, and he knows what he is about.

There are two ways in which healthy survivability can develop in silent sons. On one hand, there are boys who come through incredibly troubled families and still emerge as healthy men. Although this does not happen very often, a number of researchers have found that at least 10 percent of children from severely dysfunctional families emerge as healthy people.[1]

The explanation for this includes getting help from outside of the family, having a positive attitude or temperament, resiliency in the face of stress, and the ability of some children in dysfunctional families to have a sense of autonomy.

On the other hand, I believe that men can become healthy survivors by using their strengths and positive characteristics to overcome their pasts. This type of man knows that what he has learned from his experience is more important than where he has been. He builds on his experiences and does not allow them to tear him down. While it may seem that the term "healthy survivor" describes a man who is not affected by anything, this is not true. The healthy survivor does not deny his experiences, nor does he let them force him into negative behaviors. Rather, he has learned to maintain balance in himself and his life. If he is in pain, he deals with it. He admits when he is vulnerable, and is able to ask for help. He is not afraid to show his emotions, but he is not controlled by them either. He knows he is in control of himself. More importantly, he likes who he is and is comfortable with his life. It may have taken a long time for him to grow into a healthy survivor, or he could have been using his strength all along. Either way, the healthy survivor would not trade places with anyone today. He values what it took to get him where he is and he values himself. He is not for sale.

Healthy survivors share many positive traits. How many of the following do you have?

- He knows how to attract and use the support of healthy people around him.
- He has developed a healthy sense of humor.
- He has developed a well-balanced sense of autonomy.
- He is socially at ease and others are comfortable around him.
- He is willing to identify and express his feelings.
- He can work through, not deny, his problems.
- He is neither controlled or controlling.
- He does not live in fear of his past, but with contentment and a sense of power about the present.
- He can love and be loved.
- He likes who he is, not what he is.

If you are like me, you probably identified with more than one of the types. While I was growing up and as a young man I fit into the achiever and the hypermature patterns. I am sure that at 16 I was so hypermature it was sickening. I behaved as if I invented responsibility. I'm still responsible, but my motivations are much different now. I still like to do things and I am proud of my achievements. But now I like myself too. I feel good about being male, a silent son, and a man. I hope now I am closer to being a healthy survivor. It took some effort to get to this stage, and along the way there were many struggles, failures, fears, doubts, and long days. Along the way there was one thing that held me back, as it does so many other silent sons. This one thing burdens us like a heavy unwanted blanket. Unless we kick it off, it will destroy us. This one thing is—anger.

ANGER: ONE OUTLET, MANY EMOTIONS

> *As the son of an alcoholic father, the only male role model I had growing up was extremely dysfunctional. The only emotion my father expressed with any regularity was anger. As a result, I have had to work very hard in recovery to get beyond anger and get in touch with my emotions, to identify them, and to share them appropriately with others.*
>
> DEVON

Silent sons often appear to be constantly angry. Are they really angry, or are they just using anger to hide or project other emotions? When I ask a group of men to write down their feelings, I usually get a list of five or six, typically anger, joy, frustration, happiness, rage, and contentment. Yet these men can and do possess hundreds of different emotions. I wonder if some of their anger does not come from a frustration over the inability to express themselves. It seems they put all of their emotions into one socially acceptable basket. This is particularly true when men interact with other men. A man is more likely to let another man think he is angry than to tell him he is frustrated, depressed, or hurt.

Anger is always a double-edged sword. You can be angry over your past and your anger can ruin the present. You can also be angry and have no idea why. Are you aware of the different areas in your life that are affected by your anger? Take the following anger impact inventory test to see the extent to which anger might be a part of your life, whether you know it or not.[2]

ANGER IMPACT INVENTORY

Instructions: Using the five-point scale, rate the degree of impact your anger has on the areas of your life listed below.

0 = none
1 = minor
2 = moderate
3 = significant
4 = major

1. Relationships with authorities (teachers, bosses, police, etc.) _____
2. Relationships with peers and colleagues at work _____
3. Relationships with subordinates at work _____
4. Relationships to customers, clients, business associates, and so on _____
5. Relationships to children _____
6. Relationships with children's teachers, other parents _____
7. Relationship with spouse or lover _____
8. Relationship with previous spouse or lover _____
9. Relationships with in-laws _____
10. Relationships with parents _____
11. Relationships with other family members _____
12. Relationships with current friends _____
13. Relationships with former friends _____
14. Relationships with neighbors _____
15. The role of anger in lost relationships _____
16. Relationships with recreational groups or organizations _____
17. Relationships with religious groups or organizations _____

18. Relationships with political and other groups   ———
19. Impact on your health because of anger episodes   ———
20. Effect of anger symptoms (rapid heart rate, tension, shoulder and neck pain, headache, irritability, feeling of pressure, restlessness, insomnia, brooding, stomach problems, etc.)   ———
21. Time lost due to angry feelings   ———
22. Anger intrusion into leisure activities (vacations, hobbies, etc.)   ———
23. Effect of anger on drinking or drug use   ———
24. Effect of anger on experiences while driving   ———
25. Effect of anger on your creativity, productivity, or potential   ———
26. Accidents, errors, and mistakes   ———

A score of 3 or 4 in any area above tells you that anger is having a significant impact on that part of your life. It is obvious that anger can affect many areas of your life, but what exactly does anger do for you? In the book *When Anger Hurts,* Matthew McKay and his co-authors point out that anger has four functions—they call these painful affect, painful sensation, frustrated drive, and defense to threats. All apply to silent sons.

Anger as painful affect can block other painful emotions resulting from a bad experience. It makes you unaware of what is actually happening to you. It also allows you to release intense emotions of hurt and anxiety that you might not otherwise express.

Anger as painful sensation is used to discharge stress or overcome fatigue. If you have had a very difficult experience or day, you may come home and explode. How often have you become angry because you are tired? Obviously, this kind of outburst is not healthy for you or those around you. This function of anger is also used to overcome fatigue.

Frustrated-drive anger occurs when you cannot express what you want or need. It often develops because things are not the way you think they should be, or, if you are a perfectionist, nothing is the way it should be. It also happens when you are forced to do things you don't want to do. This type of anger can be especially felt by a silent son.

Finally, anger serves as a response to a threat. When you are threatened, you want to reduce the stress and thus you become angry. As a silent son, you can feel threatened when you feel attacked, controlled by others, or abandoned.

When you want to know where you stand today, identifying with one or more of the personality types might give you a clearer picture of yourself, but where you stand on anger will determine how well you can make positive transitions in your life. If you remain silent and never seek to change, regardless of what type of silent son you are, anger will dominate your life. If you allow all of your negative emotions to be expressed behind an angry façade, you will never know yourself. You will never know your potential because it will be blocked by anger. Anger solves very little, but keeps in a lot. You strike out at others when you have been hit. Anger needs to be released if appropriate, but more importantly, it needs to be resolved.

As a silent son, where do you stand today? Do you know what you stand for as a man? You will not know what you stand for until you can see yourself clearly. Nothing will block your vision more than anger.

The healthy silent son sees more than a type. He sees more than anger. He sees his potential and *all* of his emotions. He sees himself and he likes what he sees.

AFTERTHOUGHTS

If we are strong, our strength will speak for itself. If we are weak, words will be no help.

JOHN F. KENNEDY

He was one of those men who possesses almost every gift, except the gift of the power to use them.

CHARLES KINGSLEY

Fall seven times, stand up eight.

JAPANESE PROVERB

Experience is not what happens to a man. It is what a man does with what happens to him.

ALDOUS HUXLEY

What matters is not the size of the dog in fight, but the size of the fight in the dog.

COACH PAUL BRYANT

CHAPTER FOUR

The Dysfunctional Family:
The Battle Within

All happy families resemble one another; every unhappy family is
unhappy in its own way.
LEO TOLSTOY

Over the past twenty years there has been great debate regarding the impact of the dysfunctional family on its members. There are theorists who believe that family background disproportionately affects everything in the development of a person; others maintain that it is only one of many factors that influence development; and still others insist that for an adult, family background is irrelevant. I believe the truth lies in a combination of these views.

The extreme position (i.e., it's all the family's fault) does not allow for individual response to family experiences or accepting responsibility for one's own behavior, and ignores the everyday "normal" problems we all face as men. I believe that this view cannot offer a balanced understanding of men and their families. However, I do not want to go too far in the other direction and suggest that family impact is irrelevant. We cannot deny the influence our family has on us, but we also cannot use it to excuse any and all of our behavior. For many silent sons, however, the major problem is not accepting or denying family implications on who we are today, because we are not yet fully aware of the impact that our families had on us.

If we are asked about our family of origin, we are likely to describe where we lived, what our fathers did, and maybe say something about our schools or neighborhoods. We are usually very matter-of-fact about our families. Even when there was trouble, we seldom mention it because we assume that since the experience is over so is the pain. Even if we are in pain, we seldom acknowledge that either.

Most men I talked with about their families initially exhibited what I call a "Walter Cronkite Attitude." I remember when Walter Cronkite reported the evening news, and no matter what happened that day— good or bad, wars or truces, deaths or medical discoveries, he summarized everything with "And that's the way it is." I'm sure he had myriad feelings about the world issues and people in his nightly reports, but he rarely let it show.

The only time I recall not hearing his usual closing statement was the day Louis Armstrong died. When the segment about Armstrong's life concluded, there were tears in Cronkite's eyes; he didn't say a word. The broadcast simply ended. As reporter, he always tried to keep his emotions and personal opinions to himself. Somehow it seems we all identified with him and his emotional reserve. Perhaps there is some Walter Cronkite in all men, and particularly in silent sons.

Although we may say "That's the way it is" when discussing our families, the ways in which our families influenced us cannot be dismissed. We cannot ignore the recurring problems seen in those men who come from dysfunctional families. In many cases, problems such as alcoholism, spouse abuse, child abuse, or divorce are generational. For example, we know that those who suffer abuse as children often become abusers themselves, and that children of alcoholics are four times as likely to become alcoholics. A son who witnessed spouse abuse in his family is six times more likely to abuse his spouse than a boy who grew up in a nonviolent family. Regardless of the debates about the impact of dysfunctional families, we know that dysfunctional families produce victims. We know that many of the victims are sons in pain who feel isolated and are at risk of repeating these destructive behaviors.

FUNCTIONAL VERSUS DYSFUNCTIONAL FAMILIES: WHAT'S THE DIFFERENCE?

Was I abused or was it normal?

STEVE

Not all healthy families are healthy all the time, and not all dysfunctional families are dysfunctional all the time. Each type, however, has patterns of behaving that keep it either in or out of balance. One way to determine the difference between the two types is to examine how each handles a crisis.

During a crisis the healthy family knows and uses alternatives to its usual patterns, and as a result can return to balance when the crisis is over. For example, when an argument occurs between the spouses in a healthy family, each listens and negotiates with the other. Compromise is used, the real problem is confronted, and the family returns to balance. Healthy families must be flexible to maintain balance.

A dysfunctional family's patterns are very rigid. One individual controls family decisions or dominates conversations, adherence to restrictive rules is strictly enforced, and there is absolute denial of family problems, to cite just a few examples. Maintaining these patterns during a crisis doesn't allow any alternatives to resolving it. In fact, a dysfunctional family is likely to become even more rigid during a crisis and, as a result, become even more dysfunctional. Few things are ever resolved in a dysfunctional family, and a given crisis becomes just one more unresolved issue. As a result, most dysfunctional families are in constant crisis. In an abusive family, for example, the threat of violence never goes away.

Most dysfunctional families will grow increasingly more dysfunctional unless someone seeks help. But getting help requires breaking rigid patterns, and this, of course, is against the dysfunctional family's rules. For example, many dysfunctional families engage in what is called "group think."[1] While group think maintains rigidity, it also ensures that everyone thinks alike. Some aspects of group think include:

- The family has a single-minded purpose which defies corrective action.
- The family insists on a closed information system.
- The family demands absolute loyalty.
- The family avoids internal or external criticism.
- The family welcomes you only to the extent that you conform to its beliefs and patterns.

Another major difference between functional and dysfunctional family systems involves the victimization of family members either physically or emotionally, as well as a loss of healthy opportunities for growth. Victimization is such a common theme in dysfunctional families that those from all types of dysfunctional families joined the adult children of alcoholics movement, not because they identified with alcoholism, but because they identified with family victimization. Another common theme is anger over lost opportunities, which frequently remains overlooked. We have become so obsessed with talking about victimization that we sometimes fail to understand that not only are dysfunctional family members victimized, but they also suffer from and become angry about what they *missed* while growing up in their families. For example, a silent son with a dysfunctional father not only was intimidated or abused by his father, but also missed out on the opportunity to have a healthy father-son relationship. The pain of physical abuse goes away, but pain of lost opportunity remains. In my interviews, most silent sons of dysfunctional fathers talked more about the "fathering" they missed than about their father's dysfunctional behaviors.

According to Robert Bly, poet and author of *Iron John,* for a boy to become a man he must be taught by older men who have an interest in the boy.[2] A boy needs a mentor—it could be his father, uncle, neighbor, teacher, or close friend. A true mentor is not only interested in teaching the boy the ways of men, he is also interested in the boy's "soul." Many silent sons lacked a father who was capable of being a mentor. Their souls have never had a chance to be heard.

Can you remember who taught you how to handle your emotions? Who taught you how to handle pain? Most silent sons cannot remember being taught these things. Perhaps this is because they cannot remember having a mentor. In most dysfunctional families the father is either in great pain himself or preoccupied with trying to survive someone else's pain, such as his wife's or children's. For example, when a mother is dysfunctional, it also affects how a father performs his roles. Even in those cases where silent sons state that their fathers were there for them, the family usually remained emotionally isolated from other families. In other cases where the sons had healthy relationships with their fathers, most boys still covered up what was happening in their families and were not likely to share their emotional needs with older men.

> *I could not point to any need in childhood as strong as that of a father's protection.*
>
> SIGMUND FREUD

Today many families, dysfunctional or not, are without men. The worst learning situation for a boy is when he observes his own father ignoring his responsibilities, and that includes ignoring the needs of his son. The boy is left with a negative male image that is hard to overcome and even harder to accept, because it has been reinforced by his own father. The rage that begins with the absence of the father will continue to grow if there is also the absence of a mentor.

A man who has compassion and respect for others can set a great example for a boy. To be an effective mentor, a man should spend time with a boy over a period of time, but even a "mentor moment" can be very powerful. Can you remember such a moment in your life when a mentor affected your life in such a way that you will always remember him?

During the fifth game of the 1991 World Series between the Atlanta Braves and the Minnesota Twins, Joe Cozart took his son, Joe, Jr., to the parking lot of the Atlanta stadium to soak up the atmosphere even though they did not have tickets. The series was tied (two games each) and scalpers were selling tickets for as much as $700 a seat. A stranger approached the father and son and asked them if they would like to see the game from the inside. The man gave them two tickets five rows behind the Twins' dugout. The stranger stopped by during the game to see how Mr. Cozart and Joe, Jr., were enjoying the game. When Joe and his son asked the man's name, he told them to have a good time and walked away. That day a dream came true for a 10-year-old boy in Atlanta. His life was forever touched by a kind, generous stranger.

Joe, Jr., might wonder what kind of man gives World Series tickets to a father and son he doesn't know. Somewhere in the boy's heart he knows the answer. It is the kind of man he wants to be.

Children growing up in healthy families have a feeling of completeness and wellness. Children from dysfunctional families have a feeling of loss and emptiness. "We never did that in my family" or "I never got a chance to try that" are not uncommon statements made by men from dysfunctional families. As adults, they know something is missing. Many spend most of their lives trying to find it and understand its source. Others try to pretend it doesn't exist, but they can't ignore the unexplained emptiness.

How do you know if something was missing in your family? Usually you don't, until you become aware of something different. For example, most young children who are physically abused do not consider themselves wronged until the abuse is discovered by others or until they witness how healthy families function.

Read the following list of characteristics which are often found in a healthy family. How often did healthy behaviors occur in your family? How often were they missing? Use the following scale to assess your family background while you were growing up.

1 = often
2 = occasionally
3 = rarely

1. My family communicated and listened. _____
2. My family affirmed and supported its members. _____
3. My family taught respect for others. _____
4. My family developed in me a sense of trust. _____
5. My family had time for play and humor. _____
6. My family exhibited a sense of shared responsibility. _____

7. My family taught me right and wrong. _____

8. My family observed rituals and traditions. _____

9. My family had an equal balance of interaction among its members. _____

10. My family shared a sense of values. _____

11. My family respected privacy. _____

12. My family valued service to others. _____

13. My family fostered honest conversation. _____

14. My family shared leisure time. _____

15. My family admitted problems and sought help. _____

16. My family appreciated children. _____

17. My family had many outside friends. _____

18. My parents liked each other. _____

Now add up your score. The higher your score, the more that was missing. The more that was missing from your family, the more likely it was dysfunctional. You might come from a dysfunctional family, but you may have still have experienced some of the healthy behaviors above. Just as healthy families are not healthy all the time, dysfunctional families are not dysfunctional all the time. Families are dysfunctional by degree. Also, the more dysfunctional the family, the fewer of the child's needs are met. Behaviors necessary for a healthy childhood are missing in a dysfunctional family. In fact, in most dysfunctional families, *childhood* is missing.

CHARACTERISTICS OF DYSFUNCTIONAL FAMILIES

A dysfunctional family is a family that has a problem but won't do anything about it. The problem might include any of the following:

alcoholism	divorce
child abuse	spouse abuse
emotional abuse	emotional neglect
severe parental fighting	spouse infidelity
compulsive gambling	religious rigidity
workaholic parent	criminal behaviors
drug addiction	

73

Obviously, there are many other problems seen in dysfunctional families which can be added to the above list. Also, most dysfunctional families rarely suffer from just one problem. Usually it is a combination of several, although all may be related to a single source, such as violence. Regardless of the originating problem, dysfunctional families appear to share certain characteristics. These are the characteristics which contributed to how your family became dysfunctional, and which contributed to the memories you are trying to overcome.

PARENTAL FIGHTING

> *I was frequently caught between my mother and father. They would often fight in the evenings. I would usually get pulled in, and then later at night when they would "make up" I would still be left full of frustration.*
>
> NORMAN

According to the psychologist Nathan Ackerman and his theories on family therapy, the number-one indicator of a dysfunctional family is the relationship between the parents.[3] When spouses are involved in a troubled relationship, it detracts from their parenting skills. How well your parents got along with each other laid the foundation for the kind of family life you had. Especially important was your perception of how well they got along, because that became the basis by which you responded to your parents' temperament. When parents are fighting with each other it creates a "cold war" atmosphere and children walk around on eggshells. Can you remember times when you just wanted your parents to stop fighting? Did you do things you believed would keep them from fighting, eventually realizing that your efforts seldom worked?

Mine and other studies have found that children are very interested in helping their parents get along better. For example, in one study, 96 percent of young children of alcoholics ranked the arguing and fighting between their parents as a greater problem than the drinking.[4] In my work with adult children of alcoholics, I found that sons of alcoholics ranked getting their parents to get along better a higher priority than getting them sober.

Silent sons were very aware of their perceptions of their parents' relationships. In fact, only 11 percent of those I surveyed perceived that their parents had an above-average relationship. But 40 percent of men from functional families perceived their parents' relationships to be above average.

PARENTS AS VICTIMS

Since many of the problems of dysfunctional families are generational, it is highly likely that one or both of your parents were victimized. It is easier to understand your parents when you begin to learn things about them and especially about their childhoods. If you seek to better understand who you are today due to the impact of your childhood, I challenge you to try to better understand your parents by learning something about their childhoods. This won't encourage you to accept their dysfunctional behavior, but it will help you to know the potential sources of it.

When you are in pain, you seldom consider your parents' pain. You question their behavior, but not its source. You think they act in a vacuum. But just as you bring your family experiences with you into adulthood, so did they.

Phil, age 48, an auto body worker and a father of two children, talks about his boyhood and his father. "When I was a boy I loved Christmas. My father, however, rarely participated in the usual rituals of getting a tree, and decorating it or the house. My mother and I did these things. My mother always liked the house decorated for Christmas and I knew she was pleased when it was done.

As the years passed, we would make light of his lack of participation. In response, he would usually smile and tell us he didn't want to take all the fun away from us. By the time I was in high school I did most of these things by myself. As an only child I enjoyed it, but I knew there was something missing. After all, wasn't Christmas supposed to be a "family" time? I had watched all the black-and-white Christmas movies; you couldn't fool me.

It was not until years later that I began to understand why my father didn't want to take part in the holidays. The secret was in his past. My father had a very tough life as a boy. My grandfather was a very rigid and demanding man. Life for my father, my uncle, and my grandmother was very difficult and very painful. While I was growing up my father rarely talked about his father, and when he did it was usually with anger. However, you always find out about people in your family from someone. Gradually I was able to piece some family history together.

Christmas for my father had been just one more troubled time in his life and a clear reminder of what was "missing" in his childhood. In fact, by the time my father was 8, his family "quit" having Christmas. My grandfather figured since the boys knew the truth about Santa Claus there was no reason for presents. I learned that one Christmas, my father wanted a pair of shoulder pads for football. That particular Christmas there was no tree, no decorations, and no mention of Christmas. When he awoke on Christmas morning, there was a pair of shoulder pads on the kitchen table. They weren't even wrapped.

My father never complained about his boyhood to me. Like most men of his time, he kept it to himself. I always figured my father didn't decorate the tree because he thought it was for women and children. Later, I thought maybe he was uncomfortable decorating a tree. Now I realize two things about him. One, he probably really didn't know how to decorate for Christmas. Two, and most importantly, Christmas time was a very painful time for my father. Every Christmas reminded him of the past. I never would have considered my father's pain a reason until I began to learn more about him.

Childhood for both of us is over, but as men, and, as father and son, we have grown closer. He let me in by talking about his childhood. I let him in by learning about him. Holidays are different for us today. My parents never miss Christmas at our house with our three children. My father always comments about the beauty of the tree, and I have a real picture, both on paper and in my mind, of my father helping to decorate."

ROLE REVERSAL

Role reversal occurs in dysfunctional families when children are expected to act like adults, take care of their parents, or take over the duties of the parents, such as caring for siblings. Did you ever "fill in" for your dad? Were you ever expected to be the "man of the house"? Role reversal also occurred when you had to alternately be a child, take on the role of an adult, and then revert back to being a child.

In highly abusive families it is not uncommon for a parent or parents to believe that the child is there to meet their needs. The child is supposed to make the parent feel fulfilled or happy. How often have you heard people say that a couple needs children to be complete, or that having a child will save a troubled marriage? Usually the reverse happens, and the added stress and responsibility only hasten the collapse of an already weak relationship. Then, too often, the parents blame the child. I have heard too many sons tell me they were born to save their parents' marriage, but their father left anyway. What does this mean to the child? Does it mean the child wasn't good enough and it's his fault his father left and his mother is unhappy? No, but unfortunately these are the messages that children receive.

Another common pattern of role reversal is called "emotional incest." It occurs when a son is asked to be an emotional confidant for one or both of his parents. In dysfunctional families people might talk about the problems, but rarely to the right person.

If a father is physically and emotionally unavailable to his wife, she might enlist her son as her confidant. Usually when this happens the son is uncomfortable around his father, and the father can guess that things are being said behind his back. This could lead to open warfare between father and son. After all, how do you feel when you think someone knows more about your problem than you do? The father could also be embarrassed and take it out on the son. It is a no-win situation.

I am not talking about helping a parent for healthy reasons. I am talking about things like cleaning up after a parent who drinks too much, or paying the bills for an irresponsible mother or father, and making excuses for why he or she can't go to work.

I *am* talking about a parent taking on the responsibilities of the other parent. Even though we believe that both parents are equally responsible for the family, children still expect each parent to maintain certain responsibilities. In dysfunctional families, role reversal upsets the system, creating resentment among family members, like when a mother fulfills a father's role and a boy knows that it should be his father spending time with him or teaching him. The boy resents the absence of his father, the mother resents the additional duties, and the father often later resents that someone has taken his place. This leads not only to role reversal, but also to role confusion about who does what, and to role strain when one person is asked to do too much. Each member of a family has a certain role, and no one member should play all the roles. It's tough enough to be a son, let alone your own parent or, worst of all, your parents' parent.

PROGRESSIVE LOSS OF SELF-ESTEEM

> *Why do so many of us have such low self-esteem? Does lack of faith in ourselves come from lack of self-esteem?*
> CALVIN

I believe the most significant negative impact on a child of a dysfunctional family is loss of self-esteem. This can occur in a variety of ways, but the end result is usually the same. Namely, many dysfunctional families produce silent sons who don't like themselves. This is a terrible handicap. It is very difficult to expect other people to like and love you when you don't like what you are offering them.

Loss of self-esteem can happen if, as a child, you never believe that you are good enough. It can happen as a result of parental rejection. It can happen if you can't "make" your family healthy, and thus feel like a failure. It can happen because you blame yourself for the trouble in your family. Finally, it can happen because you feel compelled to do things that you do not want to do, things that make you feel badly about yourself.

Can you remember doing things in your family that you did not want to do? Can you remember how you felt about it? Can you remember saying to yourself, "I shouldn't have to be doing this, this isn't right, this isn't normal?" Were you talking about picking up or cleaning up after someone, listening to emotional outrages of parents, or going to family counseling? Did you often feel hurt, did you cry, fear your father, or hide alcohol from a parent? As you got older, did you find yourself feeling guilty but not knowing why? Did you ever start losing respect for yourself?

Our self-esteem can drop when we believe we are not acting like a "real man." Living in a dysfunctional family can contribute to our having to do many unmanly things, such as lying to cover up for our parents or hiding from a parent because of fear. This doesn't mean that men don't do these things, but rather that being forced to do them affects our self-image, which in turn affects our self-esteem.

Usually the loss of self-esteem in a dysfunctional family is progressive, and we are therefore not aware of it. As boys, one day we turn around and realize that we don't feel good about ourselves. We feel pain, but we don't know the source of that pain. We are sure that we have done our best, that we have done more than is expected of us. "Surely," we rationalize, "this makes me a good person." So why don't we feel good about ourselves? Usually it is because we have lost ourselves. Little by little, who and what we are becomes less important than the problem in the family.

In a dysfunctional family, everyone comes second to the problem. It is difficult to develop and maintain a high self-esteem when you are treated as inferior to the problem. You want to rage against the obvious—"I'm more important than Mom's drinking, I'm more important than his compulsive gambling, I'm more important than your stupid arguments!"—but when no one listens, you begin to doubt it yourself.

INCREASED TOLERANCE OF INAPPROPRIATE BEHAVIOR

Dysfunctional families teach you to tolerate things you never thought you could. If you stay a member of the family and are part of "group think," you learn to tolerate behaviors because others around you do the same. Most tolerance builds up over time as the dysfunction progressively gets worse. You find yourself hoping it will change, and while you wait you tolerate the behaviors.

Tolerance of inappropriate behaviors leads you to lower your expectations of normal behavior. If you can't reach the goal of having a successful or happy family, you can either try harder or alter the criteria of success by lowering your expectations. For example, in alcoholic families, instead of demanding change or seeking help you often hear: "At least he isn't drinking today, isn't that great?" No, it isn't great. It means you have given up by learning to settle for less.

Once you learn a high tolerance for inappropriate behaviors, you are at high risk of continuing the pattern in your own adult relationships. You are at high risk of being used by others and having them take advantage of you. This can occur in your romantic relationships, at your job, and in your friendships. You can even begin tolerating your own inappropriate behavior.

If you tolerate inappropriate behaviors in others, you simultaneously learn to expect that others should tolerate the same in you. Many silent sons become angry and aggressive. They, too, can engage in inappropriate behavior, but because of their backgrounds they see nothing wrong with how they act and they expect others to tolerate them. Thus the cycle of dysfunction is fostered and continues.

CHRONIC TENSION

As a family becomes more dysfunctional, tension grows. Eventually it gets to the point where it is always present. The difference between low and high tension is only a drink or an argument away. Everyone wants to deny that something is wrong in the dysfunctional family, but no one is happy. Did you ever walk out of your house and release your tension with a sigh? It's like a silent message to yourself: "Boy, am I glad I'm out of there." Getting out of the house even for a little while becomes a way to break the tension.

I call tension in the family the "walking-on-eggshells syndrome." Everyone is afraid to speak out or to be themselves for fear of an explosion. Even in good times, smiles are measured and everyone is emotionally on guard.

Dysfunctional families are especially tense, not only because of the dysfunction but also because of the associated behaviors. Abuse, addiction, or violence is always accompanied by a tense silence. Conflicts are never resolved, and the tension becomes the bridge to the next episode.

Warren, 34, remembers the constant tension in his house. He was always waiting for what was going to happen next, always expecting the worst. He states, "Although I wasn't physically abused, I felt abused mentally; I was humiliated, and I felt shame. I remember sitting in the car outside the bar my father ran into for 'a minute' but it turned into two hours. I wanted to walk home, but I was afraid to betray him. I was stuck with feeling frustrated, and always being told, "Don't tell your mother." And she would always quiz me when we arrived home late.

It is no wonder that many silent sons find it so hard to relax as adults. In fact, one of the most difficult places for many silent sons to relax is with their own families. We are not used to things being calm or stable. Surely, we believe, something is going to go wrong, and we remain tense until it happens. Also, we provoke it with our tension.

THE BATTLE WITHIN

Dysfunctional families exhibit other characteristics, such as denial, rigidity, inconsistency, self-blame, lack of trust, poor communication, and emotional isolation. If you were raised in a dysfunctional family you may recognize many of these characteristics.

What do you do with the issues of the past? Who is responsible for old problems and who owns the solutions?

There is a growing backlash of people trying to blame their problems on their parents. I do not *blame* parents for the problems of their adult offspring, because as adults we must take responsibility for our lives. However, I cannot *excuse* some of the things that parents in dysfunctional families do to children. There are far too many children killed and seriously injured by their parents. There are too many children who suffer so much at the hands of their parents that they are not capable of leading healthy adult lives. Also, if you come from a dysfunctional family, you may be creating a dysfunctional family of your own right now.

The purpose of understanding your dysfunctional family is not to find blame, but rather to understand yourself and find resolution. Most men are not accustomed to blaming others anyway. For example, a player gets "racked up" in a football game and is carried off the field. You don't see him ranting and raving up and down the sidelines demanding to know who on the other side is responsible for his injury. Oh, sure there are grudges settled on the field, but generally the player is more interested in recovering so that he can get back into the game. He understands the risk of injuries and considers them part of the game. Some players play even when hurt, but they know they play better when they are totally healthy. The same is true for silent

81

sons who want to get on with their lives. They want to get back in the game. This does not mean that they don't protect themselves. The man who knows he is vulnerable and uses healthy practices to protect himself reduces his vulnerability. Blaming our parents keeps us stuck in the past. Finding solutions keeps us living in the present. We must not deny our pain, however. Finding solutions just means we don't have to go on in pain. And it doesn't mean we are not entitled to grieve our losses.

Men raised in dysfunctional families have suffered many losses. They need to grieve them. Robert Bly says there is great grief in men's lives and few of us acknowledge it.[5] As silent sons we have survived the wars of our dysfunctional families, but the fighting goes on within us. We are fighting against admitting our pain, against admitting the truth about our families, and against ourselves. We don't even want others to know we are struggling. We dismiss our childhood by shouting: "It was OK!" Well then, what does it take to make it not OK? How much is too much?

Maybe Walter Cronkite was right: "That's the way it is." But just because that's the way it was yesterday does not mean that's the way it has to be tomorrow. It doesn't mean that's the way it has to stay. Our dysfunctional families tell us where we have been. Do they also have to tell us where we are going? Don't we have a choice, or are we so unconscious of our situations as men and silent sons that we never think about looking at ourselves any other way?

Do you take your past and yourself for granted? Think about it. Doesn't being taken for granted mean you do what others expect of you but get no recognition? You think it's your duty or your job. Men may be so taken for granted that they never even consider that they are being taken for granted. Take a boy, for example. You raise him, tell him when he becomes a young man that he will take a job for the next fifty years of his life, work at it every day, and this is what is expected of him. You can tell him that when he is 18 he can be sent by his government off to war if his government so chooses. Few of us ever question these things, so why should we question such a small thing as a dysfunctional family?

Most of us accept conflict and tension in our families without question. We cannot consider alternatives, because we have not developed a consciousness about ourselves. No movement, be it self-help, recovery, women's or men's, could have ever begun until a certain level of consciousness was reached. Silent sons have a right to be aware of their pain and to try to understand it.

We do not study dysfunctional families to find out whom to blame. We study dysfunctional families to find out where to begin to change our lives. What needs to be changed? What can we keep? What losses do we cut? It's time to get on with our lives and stop taking ourselves and our past for granted. We can't take others down in order to build ourselves up. We can, however, acknowledge the impact others have had on us in order to find not only who we are but also where we want to go. Learning more about ourselves as boys and about our families allows us to learn more about becoming healthy men. We are all starting a journey. When we were young, some of us were given the wrong maps. It is time to make our own way and make our own maps. The road to health and safety does not include traveling over and over again back to where you have been before, but it helps to know the wrong direction and the dangers of the paths of the past. The battle is no longer behind us. The battle is now within.

AFTERTHOUGHTS

The ultimate measure of a man is not where he stands in moments of comfort and convenience, but where he stands at times of challenge and controversy.
MARTIN LUTHER KING, JR.

That which does not destroy me, makes me strong.
FRIEDRICH NIETZSCHE

Even in the deepest sinking there is the hidden purpose of an ultimate rising. Thus it is for all men; from none is the source of light withheld unless he himself withdraws it. Therefore, the most important thing is not to despair.
HASIDIC SAYING

Be willing to have it so; acceptance of what has happened is the first step to overcoming the consequences of any misfortune.

WILLIAM JAMES

God must have realized humans need to be connected with the past, so he gave us memories.

MIKE RUHLAND

CHAPTER FIVE

Boyhood: Spirit versus Silence

When childhood dies, its corpses are called adults.
BRIAN ALDISS

Erik Erikson believed that the greatest crime of humanity is to destroy the spirit of a child.[1] He believed that not only does this destroy the child, but also that adulthood is built on the spirit of childhood. If the boyhood spirit is lost, the man can spend his life trying to find it. If the boyhood spirit is wounded, the man can spend a lifetime trying to recover from his wounds. It may be hard to recover from physical harm, from loss of security, or income, or family members, but recovery from a broken spirit is the hardest of all.*

What is this thing called "spirit"? It is hard to define and difficult to measure, but it does exist. Boyhood spirit is a combination of self-esteem, a positive mental attitude, a belief in yourself, and a strong sense of identity that cannot be easily defeated. When you have spirit you are fully engaged in what you are doing. You hold nothing back. Without spirit you go through the motions of your life. With spirit you *are* life.

Remember when you played games as a boy and gave it all you had?

*All of the anonymous quotes in this chapter are from teenaged boys in dysfunctional families who are currently trying to save their spirits.

If you dove for a pass in football, you hung in the air and stretched to the limit, reaching for all you were worth. When the spirit is damaged you always seem to be holding back.

We know that spirit exists, but it has been largely ignored by psychologists studying why some people can endure hardship and still remain healthy. We've all known boys who were raised under very difficult circumstances yet were always upbeat and grew up to be healthy men. What was different about these boys compared to those who emerged from dysfunctional families only to carry on the dysfunction? I believe it was that the healthy ones never lost their spirit.

When men try to recover from boyhood dysfunction, it is not intervention or treatment or the analysis of victimization that allows them to heal, rather it is re-creating or finding their lost spirit. There can be no growth or recovery without spirit. In fact, in certain recovery programs when growth occurs it is called a "spiritual awakening."

I believe that as men today we are missing not so much our childhoods as our childlike spirits. It is also interesting to note that a vital part of many adult recovery movements includes trying to rediscover the "inner child" in each of us. The inner child concept has been a part of psychology for years. During the past ten years, however, it has been applied more than ever. This is especially helpful to those from dysfunctional families who realize their childhoods were very painful and who are trying to understand themselves better by examining the foundation upon which they are built.

Most men are not comfortable with things that are childish. The inner child concept is not childish. It is not about doing childish things. It is not about sitting in an auditorium listening to someone telling you to close your eyes and hug your teddy bear. Identifying with your inner child means finding your childhood spirit when it is lost. It is finding the soul of the boy Robert Bly talks about.

I have often wondered if many silent sons aren't on a merry-go-round of accomplishments, or crises, trying to find the meaning in their lives that escaped when their spirit died an early death. Have you ever thought that if you don't feel good about yourself today, what is bothering you is not your job, your relationships, or the mortgage, but an old wound? Childhood may be over, but childhood wounds can still be felt in adulthood. Maybe the real problem is not that these wounds didn't end when childhood was over, but that they ended childhood for you. You and your wounds were forced to adjust, and part of the adjustment was to give up being a child. You know you had a childhood and know you were an adolescent, but you also feel you missed the experiences of being a child. This child is trapped in an adult body, screaming for recognition, screaming for freedom, and in silent sons, screaming for healing. Can you hear the screams? Can you see yourself as a boy in pain, and now as a man in pain? Probably not. We seldom see these things in ourselves until we have a reason to look. We are probably all like the heroes we had when we were boys.

Can you remember your heroes? Who were they? What made them heroes? A typical boyhood hero had this profile: He was usually extremely competent at something, always saved the day, presented a super-manly image, exuded strength around women, and rarely stayed around to receive thanks. The hero was usually in some pain about his past too, but he always tried to hide it. A classic hero was the Lone Ranger. He did many good deeds, grieved for the murder of his brother, and left before anyone could ever thank him. Remember "Who was that masked man?" What made the typical hero attractive to others was his ability to be so good and strong while something was hurting him. Superman was super for everyone else, but he was only Clark Kent to himself. Maybe the "S" on his outfit really meant silent and kryptonite was really an old wound. Heroes and old wounds often go together. But it is not their wounds that inspire us, it is their spirit. The true hero grows with his spirit. The wounded hero only helps with everyone else's. Which are you?

THE WOUNDED SPIRIT

A boy's world is dominated by his family, and if the family is wounded so is the boy. Aside from your troubled family, there are several common ways in which you may have been wounded. Each wound suppresses the spirit and makes it quieter. If the wounds are too numerous, the spirit becomes silent.

GROWING UP TOO FAST

When you are forced to grow up too fast, your emotions develop ahead of your body. You are raised on emotional overload. David Elkind, a child psychologist, refers to growing up too fast as the "hurried child syndrome." Victims of the hurried child syndrome are raised under too much pressure to succeed, achieve, and please. Elkind states, "Like adults, they [children] are made to feel they must be survivors, and surviving means adjusting—even if the survivor is only four or six years or eight years old. . . . hurried children are forced to take on the physical, psychological, and social trappings of adulthood before they are prepared to deal with them."[2]

The major contributor to the hurried child syndrome is pressure, and dysfunctional families are families under constant pressure. A boy in a dysfunctional family is pressured into roles that he not only doesn't want, but also is not prepared to handle. Often he finds himself in role reversal, taking care of the parent. Many silent sons remember their roles as parent, partner, status symbol, family therapist, or family conscience. They remember very little about being a child. In my interviews one of the most common statements heard from silent sons was, "I don't remember much about my childhood." Yet most of them reported very vivid memories about all of the adult things they had to do. They remembered the pressure and the family dysfunction. Their boyhood memories were filled with their own adult behaviors. What they didn't remember about being a boy was being a child.

Silent sons often became surrogate parents not only to their parents, but also to themselves and their siblings. As boys, most remember that they took care of themselves most of the time. Relying completely on yourself means keeping things to yourself. It also means being lonely.

Matt, 15, is currently living in a boys' group home. He is trying to put his life back together after getting into trouble with drugs. He told me about his troubled family. "My mother is a prostitute and she sells her body. She always said she sold her body just to get things for us, but that wasn't true. She would get things she wanted, alcohol or drugs or whatever. I would never stand up to my mom. I was afraid to. When I was 12 or 13 I started running away a lot; I was tired of getting beat around. The last time, the cops brought me back and she was drunk and went after me. I went to bed and she came in and stabbed me with a screwdriver. After that I just left, I couldn't take it anymore."

The silent son is pressed to subjugate his own interests to those of the family. He is pressured to cover up what he is asked to endure. He is pressured "not to rock the boat" in order not to add to the existing problems. He is pressured to behave and speak like an adult while his feelings are those of a boy. He is pressured into shutting down his feelings, impulses, normal boyhood behaviors, and his spirit. He is pressured to grow up fast, while his spirit slowly dies.

During adolescence this pressure can build to enormous levels. Adolescence is a time of intense emotions. Unfortunately, when the emotions and the pressure get to be too much, many adolescents attempt to find relief by taking their own lives. In fact, suicide is the third leading cause of death among teenagers. It is often difficult to notice when the teenage boy can no longer handle emotions that are suppressed. As long as he is going through the motions every day, others may not notice the decline in his spirit.

The following poem was written by a 15-year-old boy.

A READING IN UNLOVE

Once on a yellow paper with green lines he wrote a poem.
And called it "Chops" because that was the name of his dog.
And that's what it was all about.
And his teacher gave him an "A" and a gold star.
And his mother hung it on the kitchen door and read it to all his aunts.
And that was the year Father Tracy took all the kids to the zoo and let them sing on the bus.
And that was the year his baby sister was born with tiny fingernails and no hair.
And his father and mother kissed a lot.
And the girl around the corner sent him a Valentine filled with kisses.
And his father always tucked him into bed at night and he was always there to do it.

*Once on white paper with green lines he wrote a poem and called it
"Autumn" because that's what the name of the season was.*

And that's what it was all about.

And his teacher gave him an "A" and told him to write more clearly.

*And his mother never hung it on the kitchen door because the door had
just been painted.*

*And the kids told him Father Tracy smoked cigars and put the butts on
the pew.*

*And the girl around the corner laughed when he went to see Santa Claus
at Macy's.*

And the kids told him why his parents kissed a lot.

And his father never tucked him into bed at night.

And he cried for him to do it.

Once on paper torn from his notebook he wrote a poem.

*And he called it "Question Mark Innocence" because that was the name
of his girl.*

And that's what it was all about.

And his professor gave him an "A" and a strange steady look.

*And his mother never hung it on the kitchen door because he never
showed it to her.*

*And that was the year that Father Tracy died and he forgot how the
Apostles' Creed went.*

And he caught his sister necking on the back porch.

And his mother and father never kissed any more and never talked.

*And the girl around the corner wore too much make up and that made
him cough when he kissed her, but he kissed her anyway.*

And at 3 A.M. he tucked himself into bed, his father snoring loudly.

That's why on the back of a pack of matches he tried another poem.

*And he called it "Absolutely Nothing" because that's what it was all
about.*

And he gave himself an "A" and a slash on each damp wrist.

*And he hung it on the bathroom door because he couldn't reach the
kitchen.*

Two years after writing this poem, this boy took his life.

TOO MUCH PAIN

> *My father was punching me and slapping me around
> and I just couldn't take it and I started hitting him back
> and he just looked at me. He made the comment, "You
> shouldn't have done that and you know what you are
> going to get now." He just picked me up and threw me
> down the steps and I got up and was crying. I didn't
> know what to do.*
>
> CRAIG

Nothing kills a boy's spirit better than pain. Whether it is physical, emotional or both, it attacks the spirit. His spirit can literally be beaten out of him. For example, compared to men raised in nonalcoholic families, men raised in alcoholic/dysfunctional families were six times more likely to have been physically abused, thirteen times more likely to have witnessed spouse abuse, five times more likely to have been sexually abused, and three and half times more likely to have been emotionally abused.

Many silent sons experienced much pain by watching the pain of others. One of the most common things stated by silent sons from abusive families was how frustrated and helpless they felt when their fathers were beating their mothers. As boys they were not capable of stopping their fathers. As teenagers many silent sons tried, and as a result violence was forever present between them and their fathers. Spouse abuse is not only an act of violence against a husband or wife it is also a form of child abuse. If you hurt someone a child likes and loves, you hurt the child.

Sexual abuse is the least talked about form of abuse. It is not uncommon to hear silent sons talk about how they were physically abused, but rarely that they were sexually abused. Shame creates silence. Shame kills spirit. The boy who has been sexually abused has been robbed. His innocence has been painfully taken and his boyhood is forever changed. The great pain he has been subjected to is often intensified by strong feelings of shame.

A boy can only take so much and then he must adjust. Adjustment can include acting out, engaging in self-defeating behaviors, compulsive achievement, or emotional withdrawal. Emotional withdrawal occurs when the boy tries to emotionally disassociate himself from what is happening to him or around him. He reasons, "If I don't get too close, I can't get hurt." He tries to separate his mind and emotions from what his body is experiencing. It is an admirable attempt to cope, but it doesn't eliminate the pain. It only postpones it. When he shuts down his emotions to turn off his pain, he also shuts down his spirit.

LOSS OF SELF-ESTEEM

In a dysfunctional family a boy's self-esteem is under constant attack. If you had positive self-esteem as a boy you should have been able to:

- feel you were important to someone who was important to you;
- feel "special" even if you couldn't put your finger on what made you feel that way;
- feel you were on top of things, getting done what was needed, and feeling confident that you could handle whatever came your way;
- feel purposeful—that is, working toward goals which were important to you and which expressed your own beliefs and values.

For most silent sons, maintaining positive self-esteem was a constant challenge. We often felt we were one person in the house and another outside of the house. In the house we became quiet, frustrated, angry, or depressed. Outside the house we tried to escape these feelings. We tried to keep the two separate, but the more dysfunctional the family, the harder this was to do. Some of us were able to find a balance between these disparate identities. Others found that the struggle only added confusion to the mixed messages we were already receiving from our families. It is difficult to develop and maintain positive self-esteem when you do not feel good about your family. It is difficult to develop your self-esteem when many of your role models have low self-esteem. For example, it is not uncommon for many alcoholics, abusers, gamblers, or those with other self-defeating behaviors to have low self-esteem. Additionally, those who are married to them usually suffer self-esteem loss.

Parents with low self-esteem can affect their children in several ways:[3]

- Parents with low self-esteem tend to "live" through their children.
- Parents with low self-esteem are often anxious. Anxiety distorts communication.
- Parents with low self-esteem are often threatened by high self-esteem in their children, particularly when they seek independence and autonomy.
- When parents have low self-esteem they tend to see a problem or a potential problem in everything.
- Low-self-esteem parents have difficulty praising realistically and precisely.
- Parents with low self-esteem tend to give mixed messages to their children about success.

If your parents did not have positive self-esteem, they were unable to teach what they themselves did not have and thus you either learned to imitate them, or you learned on your own. Which did you do? How was your self-esteem as a boy? Is it the same now?

THE GOOD SON SYNDROME

Did you do things that you did not want to do in your dysfunctional family just to fit in? Did you go along to get along, and then resent it? Were you repeatedly told during a family crisis: "Just be a good boy"? If so, you probably fell into the "good son syndrome." Contrary to popular belief, many sons from dysfunctional homes are not behavioral problems. In fact, in alcoholic families it was found that 80 percent of the children are incredibly compliant. In order to comply, however, you have to go along with many rules which are not healthy. For example, the good son syndrome requires the boy to:

- identify more with his parents' dysfunctional feelings than his own healthy ones;

93

- assume responsibility for things he is not prepared to do;
- act as counselor/confidant to his parents;
- pretend that everything is fine;
- not bring any of his own problems home;
- be happy all the time;
- develop a sense of maturity beyond his years;
- exchange his spontaneity and spirit for seriousness and tension.

In his book *Fire in the Belly,* Sam Keen talks about how living in a dysfunctional family can cause you to behave in ways that you do not think are compatible with being a boy.[4] It is not unusual to hear silent sons talking about picking up and cleaning up after their parents, listening to emotional outrage or hurt, and going to family counseling as boys. Additionally, many of the silent sons can remember crying from frustration, fearing their father's behavior, and attempting to comfort their mother even though they were too young to understand what was happening. All of these behaviors made them feel uncomfortable and made them feel like shouting, "I shouldn't have to do this, I am only a boy; I am a child, remember?"

However, most of us did what we thought we had to do. We did the best we could. This doesn't mean it was the best way to be a boy, and it doesn't mean we don't have feelings about it. I think indirectly we were given a choice, but we were not aware of it. Either we could have been a "good son" in a dysfunctional family—which meant doing many things we did not want to do—or we could have tried to have a good childhood, which usually involved going against the family system even though it would have been the appropriate way to develop. Most of us probably tried to do both, but felt that we did not do a very good job at either one. It is difficult to develop a whole and healthy spirit when you feel fragmented. I know there were many days that I felt pulled in two directions and I usually settled for trying to be a good son. It meant doing what was expected, not what was always appropriate for a boy.

For example, did you ever have to get your father out of a bar as a child? Can you remember walking into the bar looking for him and noticing everyone looking at you? If your father was there, it was always a difficult task to ask him to leave or to tell him, "Mom sent me." I always felt like the Roman messenger who would be killed if he delivered bad news. But you did what your mother asked you to do if you wanted to be a good son, even though this was the last thing in the world you wanted to do. Meanwhile, your mother was either waiting at home or in the car. When you returned to her, either with your father following or with the news that he was coming, it was necessary to try to be supportive of her. All of these things required you to do everything other than be a boy. You could feel your father's anger and your mother's frustration, but no one seemed concerned about your feelings.

Taking sides in your parents' arguments was another unwanted role. The good son tried to be loyal and understanding to both parents, since each parent had her or his side and wanted support. Two things were wrong here. One, parents should not force kids into taking sides. Two, you were being asked to do more than take sides— you were being asked to identify emotionally with the parent's situation. This was a parental tug of war and you were caught in the middle. There could be no winners.

> My dad came home drunk one night and my mom started cussing at him. The next thing you know he is beating her up. My mom had this .22 handgun and my dad had this shotgun. My mom went and grabbed her .22 out of her purse and she was aiming it at my dad and he just said, "OK." He went in and grabbed the shotgun and he came back to the living room. He loaded it and they both sat there cussing each other out and still fighting and pointing guns at each other. Finally, one of my brothers or sisters called the cops. The cops came flying into the house. My dad ran down the cellar and hid his gun. The cops never found him or the gun.
>
> WALT

In the average family, it is difficult enough for a boy to grow up and be called a good boy. In the dysfunctional family the concept of good takes on another meaning. Good means not what is good for the boy, but what is good for the parents. Normal boyhood behaviors are permissible as long as they remain secondary to the parents' problems. If they compete with their problems, the boy is seen as causing trouble or hard to raise. He is then caught between being a boy and being a good silent son. In order to be a good silent son, he adopts behaviors and ideas that boys in functional families seldom do.

The good son syndrome means you are good at being in a dysfunctional family. But this does not mean it is a good way to live your boyhood. Your "good" behavior can leave you with a sickly spirit.

Obviously, there are many other ways your spirit can be shattered— emotional abuse, emotional neglect, or a lack of respect, for instance. The breaking of a boy's spirit in a dysfunctional family is subtle and difficult to notice. This is because it is always part of something else—usually the dysfunction itself. A boy's spirit in a functional family can also be broken, but usually this is directly related to the boy's behavior, such as repeated failure on a team or in school. In dysfunctional families a boy's spirit gets broken as a result of someone else's behaviors. The end result is that his childhood is taken from him. It is a theft of something that cannot be replaced, one that is seldom noticed until the boy grows up and realizes what happened to him. It is not surprising that we often grieve more about our boyhoods as men than we did as boys. But while we cannot repeat our lives and relive our childhoods, we can recover our spirits.

CAUSES AND CONSEQUENCES

Our boyhood experiences can give us great insight into ourselves. We cannot dismiss our past as if it doesn't matter. Many silent sons have tried and have found that the past keeps coming back; they just repeat it in their current behaviors. Their minds have become emotional storage bins of their experiences. But it is important to remember that our dysfunctional families do not *cause* our current behaviors; we can choose to behave differently.

There is a difference between cause and correlation. Cause refers to a direct relationship between two events. It means that one event directly effects the occurrence of another. Correlation, however, means that two events frequently happen at the same time, but neither is the result of the other. It is obvious that many of the patterns found among silent sons are correlated with their past. We don't know exactly what actually causes these generational patterns, but we do know that they occur and that there are certain consequences of a boy's exposure to a dysfunctional family. For example, in her study of adult children of divorce, Claire Berman found characteristics that disproportionately developed as a consequence of the individual's having grown up in a divorced family.[5] Although the divorce was experienced during childhood, the common behaviors emerged during adulthood. For example:

- Many adult children of divorce have difficulty trusting others.
- Many fear a commitment.
- Many have difficulty with intimacy.
- Many sense themselves as isolated and lonely.
- Many struggle with problems of self-esteem.
- Many see their sexuality as a matter of concern.
- Many feel a strong need to maintain control.
- Many place a great deal of emphasis on financial security.
- Many have a strong yearning for stability.
- Many are highly empathic.
- Many are fiercely independent.
- Many place a high value on being successful.

Not all children of divorce possess the above characteristics. Similarly, not all silent sons are echoes of their childhoods. Many have gone on to live very healthy lives. These silent sons are fully aware of how they were affected and they consciously choose to make changes in their lives. They do not deny their past, but have learned from it and have moved on. There are certain experiences that we all had as boys that stay with us today. Why these experiences are so powerful or why they remain so vivid is difficult to say, but they do remain with us. They become our own folklore about ourselves. We all have a favorite tale about ourselves that we have told over and over. These stories are usually about our boyhood heroics or athletic feats, not about our pain or dysfunctional families. However, both types of stories are part of us. They are our spoken and unspoken histories.

There are moments in our lives that we keep alive forever in our minds. A boy can be touched by a moment and not even realize what is happening to him, but be changed forever. In a moment hope can be born, strength can be discovered, and love can happen. In a moment a boy can lose faith in his father, self-doubt can be created, and despair can fill his life. And in a moment a man can realize that the truth about himself lies in his childhood.

There are those who believe very strongly that boyhood experiences make the man. Avis Brenner, in her study of children and stress, says that if we can get to the child in a dysfunctional family before the age of 12 we can prevent the carryover of many of the negative effects into adulthood.[6] Unfortunately, for many silent sons the model of a man is based on what was happening to them at age 12 and how they responded to the world at that time. Mark Twain put it best: "At the age of twelve a boy starts imitating a man and he just goes on doing that for the rest of his life."

Mike is 35 and lives in Michigan. His father was not only alcoholic and abusive, but also emotionally negligent. From the time Mike was 10, what he remembered most about his father was that his father didn't want him around. "I felt that my mere presence bothered the man. He always made me feel like that. I can still picture myself doing what I thought I should do when my father was home. If I was home and my dad home I literally went to a part of the house that was the farthest from my dad. If my dad was already home when I came home I felt guilty that I had to go into the house. I never told anyone. I thought I must be doing something that he really hated."

Mike entered a support group a few years ago and began to work on his feelings. He became motivated to share his memories about not being wanted with his four siblings. After telling them how he felt as a boy, all four said the same thing: "You too? I thought I was the only one he couldn't stand!"

Mike went further with his feelings and decided to say something to his father, who was still actively alcoholic. Mike spoke to his father when he wasn't drinking and told him how he felt. He asked his father, "Just what did I do as a boy to make you dislike me so much?" His father replied, "Well, since you asked, I'm going to tell you. I don't like kids. I never liked kids. I don't like anybody's kids, you got that?"

I asked Mike how he responded to this revelation. The first thing he said to his father was, "Well, why did you have five of them?" His father didn't reply.

"What happened after that?" I asked Mike.

"Well, a real sense of anger developed in me."

"What was the source of that?" I asked.

"It was over how he treated me for so many years."

"Then what happened?"

"Well, then I started to feel a lot of resentment."

"And what was the source of that?"

"I think it was because of all the people in the world I could have gotten as a father, I got one who hated kids."

"How did you finally resolve these feelings?"

"Well, after a long time a sense of relief came over me."

"What caused that, Mike?"

He looked at me and with thirty-five-year-old tears filling his eyes said, "For the first time since I was a boy, I realized that it wasn't me."

AFTERTHOUGHTS

> *Justice was born outside the home and a long way from it; and it has never been adopted there.*
>
> WALTER CRONKITE

> *What children expect from grownups is not to be "understood," but only to be loved, even though this love may be expressed clumsily or in sternness. Intimacy does not exist between generations—only trust.*
>
> CARL ZUCKER

> *When I was a child, I spake as a child, I understood as a child, I thought as a child; but when I became a man I put away childish things.*
>
> I CORINTHIANS 13:11

> *Children have never been very good at listening to their elders, but they have never failed to imitate them.*
>
> JAMES BALDWIN

If men and women are to understand each other, to enter into each other's nature with mutual sympathy, and to become capable of genuine comradeship, the foundation must be laid in youth.

HAVELOCK ELLIS

CHAPTER SIX

Fathers and Sons:
Our Fathers Who Art in Us

Doesn't matter who my father was; it matters who I remember he was.

ANNE SEXTON

He is like no other man in the world. His influence is legendary. Without his so much as moving a finger, his look can give approval or stop you dead in your tracks. Without his saying a word, his silence says it all. He is a man who can seem capable of all feats in the world; a man who appears immortal and is supposed to live forever, or at least never grow old. He is a man of great emotions—if you could figure them out. A man of many contradictions and secrets. A man who wants to be close, but teaches independence. A man who stops hugging boys once they become 12. A man who has anger but won't tolerate it in others. A man whose physical body eventually declines, but whose emotional influence continues to grow even after he is gone. He is love, anger, rage, compassion, teacher, confusion, and strength. He is your father.

Fathers are emotionally powerful men. In fact, for their sons they are the most emotionally powerful men in their lives. You can love your father, hate him, or be somewhere in between. You can move away, be abandoned, abused, or forgotten, but you never get an "emotional divorce" from your father. Whether he influenced you positively or negatively, who he was and what he was stays with you. There is something about your father that makes him like no other man.

> *I loved my father a great deal and looked up to him with AWE—to me my father was a god. At age 14, I made a declaration to be just like him.*
>
> CLYDE

Can you remember standing next to your father or having your father walk up and stand next to you? He didn't have to say a word; his mere presence conveyed approval or disapproval. His hand on your shoulder was worth more than a thousand trophies. Standing next to your father either allowed you to feel his strength or drained the very strength from you. Standing next to your father you either felt proud and tall or small and overshadowed, but it wasn't possible not to have an emotional response. Many silent sons still respond emotionally to their fathers, even as men.

The influence of a father is universal. If we sat down and made a list of sayings and behaviors common among our fathers, I'll bet we'd find many similarities. Can't you just hear our fathers telling us:

Watch this, you might have to do this someday.
For Pete's sake, turn out the lights around here.
Who do you think you are, the King of England?
If you don't like it, Mister, there's the front door!

I was in Australia with John Lee conducting workshops for people who grew up in alcoholic families. John was curious to know if Americans and Australians shared the same father image and experienced the same fathering practices. He was greeted with some common responses to his questions, but the loudest cheers came when he asked, "Did your father have an obsession with his roof?" It seems that Australian boys constantly heard such things as: "As long as you're under my roof . . ." or "You live by my rules under my roof . . ." or "If you don't like it, get a roof of your own."

It is ironic, however, that for all of our fathers' influence and importance, we know little about them and understand even less. Fathers, fathering, and men in general have been overlooked for too long.

Silent sons, like all men, talk about their fathers, but with more confusion and emotion. In my interviews silent sons openly admitted that they were trying to understand not only their fathers, but also the influence they had had on them. In fact, unless I specifically asked about their mothers, most silent sons talked exclusively about their fathers. In many cases it appeared that the key to unlocking the son was the father.

It is not easy to reach our fathers emotionally, even when we feel the same emotions, because we don't know how to bridge the silence. Instead we settle for communication about common topics, and behaviors. For example, baseball talk between father and son is usually a "safe subject," as is other sports talk or work, because it doesn't involve any personal disclosure. It is difficult to talk about common feelings, but many sons try to reach their fathers through their behaviors and hope that somehow they can make a much-needed emotional connection.

Did you ever try to please your father by your actions? Were you really trying to gain recognition for your accomplishment, or were you hoping for an emotional response? Did you ever do what you thought he wanted and then feel that it still wasn't enough? Maybe you settled for baseball or work talk, because without these there would be no talking at all. Like other silent sons, you settled for what was safe but longed for the emotional contact.

> *I spent most of my life trying to gain his love and acceptance before I finally realized and accepted the fact that he was incapable of showing love. In trying to break the behavior pattern, I swore I'd never be like him and yet I was until I started recovery.*
>
> Doc

In dysfunctional families communication between fathers and sons is infrequent. Dysfunctional fathers cause their sons pain, because fathers absorbed in their own pain are seldom aware or willing to acknowledge the impact the dysfunction has on their sons. Therefore, it does not surprise me how much silent sons talk about their fathers. The amount of emphasis on their fathers is directly related to how much they have been hurt. Perhaps what was wounded by a father can only be repaired by a father. But what if he won't, can't, or is no longer around to fix the damage?

> *He's dead—now what?*
>
> MARTIN

The answer is that you must look to repair the wound. And the first step is confronting the truth about your father. In my work with silent sons, one of the most significant issues was wrestling with the fictional or false images they had of their fathers. When your father is dysfunctional, it is hard to admit it. You try to maintain the image of the father he was supposed to be, not the father he actually was. Eventually, maintaining a false image gets too heavy. You end up swinging in the other direction, and see your father as being dominated by his dysfunction. Neither gets you what you missed—a healthy father-son relationship.

When interviewed, all silent sons talked about wanting to have a true father-son relationship. Even if they were extremely angry and bitter, they acknowledged that at one time they wanted to be close to their fathers. In fact, much of their anger as men was because as boys they never had the kind of relationships with their fathers that they yearned for.

When a father is so dysfunctional that he cannot be a father, neither can a son be a son. He not only loses his father, he also loses part of himself. He grieves not just for the father, but also for his own losses.

Silent sons I interviewed were very much aware of these losses. Not all silent sons shared the same problems or the same images of their fathers. The issues were as varied as the attitudes held. Some silent sons possessed nothing but contempt and anger toward their fathers. Some only felt loss and grief. Some loved their fathers in spite of the dysfunction. And some expressed all of these feelings. But five common complaints stood out: (1) My father was a poor role model; (2) I never felt worthy of my father; (3) I felt under-fathered; (4) My father lacked emotions; and (5) I am afraid of becoming just like him.

POOR ROLE MODEL

I seriously doubt that when you were born someone handed your father an instruction booklet on what to do with you. Sons don't come with instructions, but men certainly come with expectations. As sons we all have unwritten expectations of what fathers are supposed to do, how they are supposed to act, and how they are supposed to feel. We expect fathers to make rules, provide economic support, teach us how to be men, show us how to treat other people, be there for our games, school plays, or band performances, comfort us when we don't do well, share our laughter, and above all, love us. During our lives we knowingly or unknowingly compare our father to these expectations. When your father lives up to them, you think you have a good father. When he doesn't, you feel cheated.

How well did your father live up to your expectations? If you are like most silent sons, you probably believe he did OK in some areas and not so well in others, but your overall opinion probably depends on how good a role model he was. Unfortunately, most silent sons had fathers who were more negative than positive role models. Their failings included not performing the functions of a father, denying a son information about being male, teaching poor parenting skills, and teaching unhealthy ways of relating to both men and women.

A FATHER'S FUNCTIONS

We can evaluate performance functionally and symbolically. Functionally, we measure the quality of the performance by how well a person performs the role. How well did your father perform the functions of a good father? If your answer is "poorly" or "not at all," then you consider him functionally deficient. Did you experience role reversal with your father and perform many of his functions for him? Did you find yourself doing things your father should have done, such as trying to fix the furnace or plumbing, making important phone calls about family matters, bringing money into the family, comforting your mother, or parenting your siblings? If so, you were like many silent sons—a child doing a man's job. When your father noticed you were handling his responsibilities, did he then correct you or criticize you? In response, you probably just kept quiet and looked at him. What could you say?

> *He was never home. I had no role model to pattern for*
> *my goals, life, or aspirations. I became an adult as a*
> *child—I was trying to fill a man's role as a kid. I had no*
> *childhood. I had to be a man. I was always ashamed,*
> *embarrassed, and angry at the world.*
>
> JIM

If your father was an alcoholic, or abusive, absent, angry, or frequently in a violent rage, then that was exactly what you had for a role model. Yet you probably would prefer to deny that those problems existed in your role model. Instead, you may prefer to say, "He was good at his job" or "Everyone in the neighborhood liked him" or "You should have seen him with a hammer and saw." But that says nothing about what kind of *father* he was. It does, however, allow you to see him with less pain, at least for a while. A father can often be excused for his weak fathering abilities if he seems strong in other areas. However, you know and feel the real truth. The only role that really matters when you are talking about your father is that special part of the man that belonged to you and only you.

> *My father's behavior was very erratic when I was 9, 10,*
> *and 11. He was physically and emotionally absent dur-*
> *ing my teenage years. I felt the lack of a role model,*
> *sought out substitute fathers, and also leaned on my*
> *mother's idea of what a man should be. I was very angry*
> *and resentful toward my father for many years.*
>
> HARRY

Symbolically, we assess a father's role not by talking about the things he did or didn't do, but by what he *meant* to you. The symbolic part of a role is extremely powerful. Most silent sons feel that their fathers were not good role models, functionally or symbolically, but find it less painful to talk about actions than feelings.

Talking about your father symbolically causes an emotional response. What happens to you when I say, "Tell me about *your father*"? Do images and emotions fill you? Are these good images and warm emotions, or do you feel rage, anger, and loss?

> *Don't mention that son of a bitch to me.*
>
> RALPH

DENIED INFORMATION

What did your father teach you? Can you list the positive and negative things you learned from him? A silent son often feels he was denied a lot of information, most importantly about what it is to be a man. Others report that if information was communicated, it was incorrect or useless. It is difficult for a dysfunctional father to teach his son positive lessons about being a healthy male. How can he teach what he does not know or understand? In my interviews, silent sons talked frequently about being denied information about sexual identity. In an average father-son relationship there is little talk about sexual identity, sexual preference, or sexual behaviors. But in a poor father-son relationship there is *no* information about these subjects, other than what is quietly observed. One of the most common questions I was asked by gay silent sons was whether or not having a dysfunctional father influenced their sexual preference. I don't know the answer to that, but when I asked them, "Do you think you would be gay if your father was functional?" the majority of the men said yes. As was true for all silent sons, the lack of information from their fathers caused them to think about the effects of having a dysfunctional father.

Lack of information causes anger in many silent sons. Do you believe that many of your problems today are the result of your not being taught what to do or being taught what is inappropriate? Do you hold your father accountable for your own negative juvenile behaviors, such as not doing well in school (because your father never paid any attention to your school work), getting into trouble (because you didn't have strong enough guidelines from him), or not feeling good about yourself (because he always put you down)? If so, it is as if you are screaming at your father: "You didn't teach me what I had to

107

know; these problems are all your fault!" It isn't all your father's fault. You are capable of learning on your own. But your rage may be keeping you from learning now what you didn't learn as a boy.

PARENTING

We learn many of our attitudes about being a parent from our fathers. The theory of transactional analysis holds that in all of us exists a parent, adult, and child. Interestingly, it is believed that the parent part is the first part developed in a human. We pick up all the rules and ideas about being a parent at a very early age.

It was not uncommon to hear silent sons talking about how their fathers' have affected their own parenting skills, the most frequently mentioned problem being lack of information about how to be a good father, which in turn leads to fear of parenting. Many silent sons would rather not have children than repeat the parenting patterns of their fathers.

RELATIONSHIPS

What did you learn from your father about being in a relationship? Did you learn healthy ways of relating to women and men? What did you learn about how to treat your partner? Did your father ever yell at you, "Don't talk to your mother like that," but he did it all the time? Did he always behave negatively in a relationship, but refuse to tolerate such behavior from others?

Many of us learned what we saw—and unfortunately, we saw two people who rarely communicated and had a relationship dominated by dysfunction. We saw a man ask his wife to tolerate a lot of inappropriate behaviors, and may have assumed that is what men do. When many of our own relationships failed, it left us bewildered. We followed behaviors that didn't work well for our fathers and didn't work well for us.

> *I came from a broken home, so I feel I don't deserve to have a good marriage because I don't know how.*
>
> GARY

108

Those of us who wanted to break the pattern may have figured out what *not* to do, but knew very little of what *to do,* having never had a positive example. The hardest thing for a father is to teach his son by positive example. The hardest thing for a son is to learn to be healthy without this example.

NOT WORTHY

Do you feel that you were never good enough for your father? I have seen many examples of fathers who, directly or indirectly, sent messages to their sons that they were simply not good enough. These messages come in many forms. Your father may assess your accomplishments, not by acknowledging them, but by comparing you to someone "better." Perhaps you play the best baseball game of your life—he'll still tell you he thinks you should be a switch hitter. You get all B's and one C on your report card, and guess which grade he focuses on? You're working at a job you really enjoy which makes you feel good about yourself, but he tells you that you don't make enough money and you're not going anywhere.

A father can make or break a son by giving or withholding approval. If you're not good enough for your father, you'll never totally believe in yourself. A man can spend a lifetime trying to gain the approval of a father who is incapable of giving it. That doesn't stop a son from trying, it just makes him push harder—and when pushing doesn't work, he gets angry at his father and himself. Think about it: Are you a son still trying to win the approval of a man who makes you angry and whose behavior does not meet *your* approval? It may not make sense, but it can make you feel like hell.

I have seen and heard many highly critical fathers talk about their sons and their sons' accomplishments with great pride and admiration. They may tell others, but they seldom tell their sons.

Ron, a 45-year-old engineer, is a friend of mine. His father, an alcoholic, was totally unavailable for Ron emotionally. He always put Ron down. Once, when we were still in college, Ron's father was talking with my father and proceeded to brag about Ron, about how well he was doing as an engineering major, how proud he was of him. My dad told me about this conversation and I remember thinking, Isn't it a shame that Ron's father can't say it to Ron? Ron's father was incapable of getting close to his son, and after many years of trying, Ron stopped wanting to be close to him.

One summer, when Ron and I were home from college, I stopped at a card store to buy my dad a Father's Day card. "Come on," I said, "You can get one for your dad too."

"No, I'll wait outside," Ron replied.

"Did you already get your dad a card?"

"No."

"Well then, come on in and get him one."

"No."

"What, you're not getting your dad a card?"

At this point I looked at my friend and saw the deep hurt in his expression. I wanted to get my father a card, even though at that time there were still a lot of unresolved problems between us. From the look on Ron's face, I knew the subject was closed.

I have heard stories like this from other sons many times. "What do you do in the card store?" they ask. All of the cards assume something about a father-and-son relationship. What happens when that relationship wasn't available to you? If you buy a card are you a hypocrite, or are you still trying to reach your father? Have you ever found a card you are comfortable giving?

Maybe you don't have to analyze the quality of your father-son relationship. Maybe you should just go into a card store and see how you feel.

If your father withheld his approval, you were probably left without guidelines. Nothing was ever good enough, so you reasoned that there must have been some unknown criteria you were supposed to follow, but no one told you what it was. No matter how well you performed, it seemed someone kept changing the "rules."

Many silent sons emerge from such confusion with standards that are even tougher than their fathers' expectations. For example, I found that among adult sons of alcoholic fathers, the three most predominant personality characteristics were taking oneself seriously, judging oneself without mercy, and constantly seeking approval and affirmation.[1] While there is nothing wrong with having high standards, there is something *very* wrong with never believing you have done your best or never feeling good about yourself.

All sons would like to make their fathers proud, but living up to your father's reputation is not living. It's a constant command performance, with no standing ovation. Dysfunctional fathers, in particular, seldom express pride, and when they do, it is usually at their son's expense. Were pride and love expressed only when you did it his way? Was he "right" *all the time?* When you were wrong, did you receive encouragement to do better, or were you put down?

I have noticed that many dysfunctional fathers are extremely argumentative, especially when they think they are right. They are quick to point out the negative in their sons, and seldom give any positive feedback. Their unconditional "rightness" leaves their sons feeling "wrong" about themselves. This pervading sense of inferiority causes their sons to stop expressing their opinions. Who wants to be told they are wrong all the time?

> *My father was full of this self-righteous crap. He was* right *all the time.* Growing up, I felt like I could never be *as good at things as he was. I was constantly afraid of him as a child. Although I hated the way he was, I turned out just like him—maybe even worse.*
>
> RUSTY

Many silent sons emerged from childhood afraid of their fathers and afraid of their own beliefs, opinions, and emotions. This left them with low self-esteem and without the security of paternal love.

When a father cannot—or will not—love his son, his lack of love creates an emptiness. There is a place in a son's heart that can only be filled by his father. When this special place is empty, the son is left to believe that he was not loved because he didn't deserve to be.

UNDER-FATHERED

Many silent sons of dysfunctional fathers suffer from being what psychologist John Friel calls "under-fathered."[2] This occurs when fathers spend little time with their sons, show little interest in their activities, and are emotionally distant or unavailable. These fathers are not able or willing to give their sons the thing they want most from their fathers—time.

Even though your father may not have been a good role model, do you feel that if you had spent more time together things would have been different? Unlike the other problems common to sons of dysfunctional fathers, this problem results not from what your father did, but from what he *didn't* do. The time that you, as a boy, could have spent with your father is gone, but the grief over the loss of your father is not.

> In my case, I didn't have an available father, so I went looking for a substitute. Of course, I thought I found one, but he was manipulative, possessive, and sexually abusive. Having no connection, or an unhealthy connection with a father or a father figure, does no good for our relationships with other men and with our own sons.
>
> TYRONE

I have found that men from functional families often talk about things they did with their fathers. Silent sons do too, but they can count the "special times" they had with their fathers on one hand. They can recall what they did in great detail. A good time with father was not an everyday occurrence.

One of my best childhood memories was when my father took me and a friend to the Pittsburgh Zoo. One summer day, he came home and I was playing with my friend Craig; we were talking about animals, and he asked if we wanted to go to the zoo. I will never forget it. We spent the whole day there. *I spent the whole day with my dad!* It was great. And he was great that day. What made this so special? That was the one and only time we ever went to the zoo.

112

As a man, I often wondered if my dad realized how great that ⟨ was or why I wished for more days like it during my childhood. May⟩ he thought kids only needed to go to the zoo once. But I knew ther⟩ was more to the man than that. Once my father called last year when⟩ I was at the movies with one of my children, who was 5. I called him⟩ back when I got home. He said, "I understand you took Bobby to the⟩ movies." "Yes," I replied, "we had a great time."

Then my father surprised me. "You're a good father," he said. And with all the warmth and greatness of that day in the zoo thirty-some years ago, he said, "I'm sorry we didn't get to spend more time like that when you were small."

"Thank you," I said, realizing that he was reaching out to me in his own way and acknowledging our shared pain over lost days. "But I'm glad we share time together now." "Me too," my father replied, knowing that the days of distance between us were over.

Too many silent sons never had even one day at the zoo. And they know they will never have the conversation with their father that I had with mine. The absence remains unfilled in their souls. It is a sadness over the bonding with their father that just never happened. Father-son bonding is something that all boys need, but it cannot occur without emotional interaction. Fathers can spend time with their sons, but unless they connect emotionally, they are merely occupying the same place and time together. Too many dysfunctional fathers are simply not emotionally available for their sons. They are usually too preoccupied with their dysfunction, and their sons come second to drinking, personality disorders, abuse, workaholism, gambling, philandering, or other such vices.

Even so, I still hear many silent sons trying to maintain the dream of closeness with their father. They try to maintain the belief that their father is a great guy because they are still hoping to fill the gnawing emptiness inside them, to connect someday. Only their father can fill this emptiness, and they know it.

Are you a silent son who always saves a place for your father at your emotional table? To satisfy your "father hunger," your father must not only show up at your table, he must also be emotionally available to you during the meal. Perhaps you, like too many silent sons, have left the table still hungry and unfulfilled.

LACK OF EMOTIONS

*Communication, trust, friendliness, anger, tension,
pride—no emotions. My father and I were unable to
conquer any of these problems until recovery, and they
are tougher now because we know what they are.*

MARK

Thus far we've talked about absent fathers and emotionally unavailable fathers, but what if your father was present? What kind of emotions did he display? Perhaps he seemed one-dimensional, or he denied his emotions. This is exactly how many silent sons described their fathers in my survey. How would you describe your father emotionally? Did he exhibit a full range of emotions, or was he primarily a one-emotion man? Did he appear to be mad all the time? Nothing and no one ever pleased him? And since no one in the family ever really knew why he was angry, did you assume it *must* have something to do with you?

When your father entered your house, what happened? Did he often bring the "big chill" with him? Too many silent sons feel that when their father was home, everyone was behaviorally and emotionally on guard to avoid setting him off. Can you remember doing this? When you were a boy, were you afraid to be yourself when your father was home?

Silent sons I interviewed were often concerned with the lack of emotions in their fathers. They talked about how their fathers often stifled their emotions, leaving everyone to guess what was going on inside them. They talked about how communication was reduced to one-word answers. There was no getting close to their fathers and their fathers were not capable of getting close to them. But the deepest hurt came from their fathers' inability to show love. Over 60 percent of the silent sons I interviewed never heard their father say, "I love you," or never got from him any display of love.

Bill, a 50-year-old computer specialist, was at a family reunion campout with as many as forty family members participating. Every night they would gather around a fire, where his father and mother would sit in

chairs at the head. The one night I was there I was admiring this family gathering, thinking how close they must be to each other. Bill's father was looking out over the entire crew with such a look of pride. Everyone was silently staring at the fire when Bill broke the silence and asked, "Dad, do you love me?" Tension filled the air. I knew I was about to witness history that night.

"What?" said Bill's father, in his why-ask-a-question-like-that voice.

"Do you love me?"

"What do you mean, do I love you? I love all my family. I raised you, didn't I? I put a roof over your head, didn't I?"

"Well then, tell me. You never told me you loved me."

At that point I realized that Bill was not going to back off. Here was a man who had come to a family gathering filled with love. He knew, however, that there was an empty place inside of him that had never been filled by his father's love. Bill was not going to live with the emptiness anymore; he needed to lay it all on the line and confront it face to face. Man to man. Father to son.

Bill got up and walked over to his father. His father stood up. No one moved. No one made a sound.

"If you love me, Dad, then tell me right now. I want to know."

Fifty years of silence was broken when Bill's father moving his massive frame reached out and pulled his son toward him. In a voice that touched all of us he said, "I love you."

This was a special moment for all the men there that night. We all knew there had been times when we needed our fathers emotionally and they either couldn't—or wouldn't—be there for us.

We were all changed that night, but Bill was changed forever. He dared to ask his father to acknowledge his love for him and his father dared to deliver.

JUST LIKE HIM

> *I once heard my mother tell my father in the middle of*
> *an argument, "You're just like your father." I swear I*
> *saw steam rising from the man.*
>
> RALPH

It is common for a young boy to say he wants to be like his father. He often looks up to his dad. A boy who has a healthy father at least has a good role model to follow, even if he chooses not to be like him when he grows up. But a son who grows up in a dysfunctional family not only lacks a positive role model, but also fears that he will become like his father. Since he often feels compelled to do exactly the opposite of what his father does, he inevitably ends up in constant conflict with him.

But what if your father also embodied some positive traits? Then you walk an even finer line. You want to follow your father's example some of the time, just not all of the time. But what do you do with your pain and hurt? You usually turn your feelings against your father, and even though he has good qualities you prefer to overlook them as a way of either getting back at him, or ensuring that you do not become like him. Still, some sons are able to selectively choose to imitate the good traits of their fathers. My own father taught me many good things, and they serve me well today. Some of his behaviors and traits I choose not to repeat, and knowing him as I do today, he doesn't blame me.

> One of the hardest things for me was to admit that the
> son of a bitch had good qualities . . . I still worry though
> that I might become like him if I'm not careful.
> FLOYD

Despite our vows to ourselves and the people we love, many of us end up realizing our worst fears. Do you feel you are becoming exactly what you don't want to be? If so, your fears may be justified.

The phrase "Like father, like son" was supposed to be a compliment, not a life sentence. Too many silent sons, however, have followed in their fathers' footsteps by becoming alcoholics, abusers, compulsive gamblers, or workaholics themselves. Why would we ever become the very thing we swore we'd never be? There are many theories which attempt to explain this, ranging from genetic to social. It may simply be that many sons repeat these patterns because it is all they know.

I believe we are most likely to repeat our fathers' behavior in a crisis situation, but even small incidents can trigger these patterns. Mostly it happens when we don't know what to do, especially in parenting situations. Then we end up sounding like our fathers. Scary, isn't it?

I also believe that some of us want so badly to connect with our dads that we inadvertently start becoming like them. Are you a silent son who does things with your father? Do you pretend to enjoy the same jokes, agree with his political views, tolerate the way he treats you and others, all in the hope of having something of a father-son relationship? But are you also drinking with him, gambling with him, and leading a miserable life with him? It may be a tough decision. Is it that if you don't do "unhealthy" things with him, you don't do *anything* together?

If you identified with any of the five issues discussed, you share this with many other silent sons. In fact, these issues were mentioned by approximately 70 percent of the silent sons I interviewed. For many the emotions were painful, but I saw many others trying to grow beyond their pain, and, as a way of doing this, trying to forgive their fathers.

Forgiving your father does not always mean confronting him and telling him that you forgive him. It means letting go of whatever he did that wounded you in your mind and heart. Forgiving your father is part of growth—maybe not his, but definitely yours. It is something you do for yourself.

Anger, rage, disappointment, and holding a grudge against your father may be prohibiting your own growth. Once you've endured this pain, you will continue to endure it if you don't learn to let it go. Am I telling you to forgive your father? No. I've heard too many silent sons tell me that some things in life are just not forgivable. I do not have the right to tell you you must forgive. *You* must make the decision if it feels right for you. But you must also examine how forgiving, or not forgiving, contributes to how you want to approach your own life.

Your decision may depend on whether or not you and your father still have "unfinished business" to attend to—if in your heart you want to tell your father, "I'm not through with you yet," you have unfinished business. Like many silent sons, you may be afraid of this unfinished business. What is it that you fear? Is it that you might have to change your image of your father? Is it that you will have to admit that he and his actions affected you? Is it that you will discover that you are just like him? Or do you fear that you still want to love him, but neither he nor you can figure out how?

We all know our fears better than we know our fathers, but we can reduce our fears by increasing how well we know our fathers and ourselves. Don't wait for your father to set you free. It's *you* who holds the key, and it's you who locks the locks.

Silent sons are capable of living a lifetime with these negative father issues still unresolved. But it's never too late to learn to let them go. It's never too late to make peace with the part of your father that you carry with you.

The following is an interview with Dan, a 70-year-old retired business executive, father, and grandfather.

ME: You have celebrated your 70th birthday this week and for many men between 30 and 50 years old, you represent their father's generation. A lot of these men are still trying to understand their fathers. Would you talk a little about men of your generation?

DAN: Well, I would say the first thing we learned was: Don't do what I do, but do what I tell you. We were also told to respect our elders, no matter who they were. If we gave a smart reply or got out of line we would get whacked. We were brought up very, very strict.

ME: Who taught you those lessons?

DAN: Mother had the responsibility, but she would always say, "Wait until your dad comes home." And, if your dad ever came into the house and Mother told him what we did, we could expect a licking.

ME: You said, "If Dad ever came into the house." Tell me a little about your family. How would you describe your family?

DAN: As far as living with my father and mother was concerned, I cannot remember enjoying my childhood at all. The best time in my early years was spent with my grandmother in the countryside. I thought she was a saint. The other big thing in my childhood was the Depression.

ME: Would you comment on the impact of the Depression on you and your family?

DAN: I was about 11 years old. Growing up in the city, the Depression had a much greater impact on me than on my wife, who grew up in the country. I can remember men on the street corner selling apples for five cents just to earn money for food. I can remember Father Cox's shantytown in downtown Pittsburgh, and I remember there were so many people jumping off the Bloomfield bridge. As a matter of fact, I remember they used to take a poll in the local bars where people would guess which days people would jump off the Bloomfield bridge. There were so many suicides. This made a great impression on me.

ME: How did your boyhood experiences influence you when you became a man? What impact does your childhood have on you today?

DAN: It has given me a much greater appreciation for the economic situation today, and having sold my business, I have sufficient money to live on and still help many members of both sides of my family.

ME: You talked about seeing men selling apples on the street. Did you ever think about how that experience influenced your ideas about men? This is not something you would traditionally see men doing.

DAN: The desperation and fear of these men was frightening. We also had very little food in our own home, and I don't know if that prompted my father to leave, but he did, for about two years. We had to move out of our very small home in the middle of the night because we couldn't pay the rent.

ME: How old were you then?

DAN: About 12. Because we couldn't pay the rent, we moved into a space above a stable that my cousin owned. He had an ice business and delivered to restaurants and bars.

ME: Who moved with you?

DAN: My mother and my brother.

ME: And your dad went where?

DAN: I have no idea. And I never asked.

ME: Your mother didn't explain where he was?

DAN: No, she didn't tell us a thing.

ME: Your father was gone for two years. Did your mother ever talk about him during that time?

DAN: No, not that I can remember.

119

ME: You mentioned your brother. Did he ever talk about your dad?

DAN: No, he didn't know anything more than I did.

ME: During the years you lived over the stable, how did your family survive?

DAN: My mother did all the bookkeeping for my cousin's ice business. His father and three brothers ran the ice business and delivered coal in the wintertime.

ME: What did you and your brother do during this time? You were in school, but did you work as well?

DAN: No, there was no work, period. We played in the streets because there were few playgrounds in the city of Pittsburgh.

ME: What about your dad? Even though he was gone, how did this make you feel about him?

DAN: Well, naturally there was a lot of resentment, there was a lot of emptiness, and of course looking back on it, I realize my mother had to do everything.

ME: I'm curious about the time before your dad left. How well did you get along with him?

DAN: Not too well. He wasn't home that much, and when he was, we had very few family conversations. He always read the newspaper.

ME: What kind of man was your father? How would you describe him?

DAN: Well, all of his business contacts liked him. As a matter of fact, he was referred to as the "mayor of Craig Street" by our neighbors in Pittsburgh.

ME: What about his behavior toward you and the rest of your family?

DAN: Are you asking about our personal feelings?

ME: Yes, yes.

DAN: Well, there was never any exchange of feelings like "We love you," or "Let's go out for a picnic, let's do something together." There was never any togetherness.

ME: Did you ever wonder why your dad was like that?

DAN: I guess I did, but I never bothered to question it.

ME: Did you think that his behavior was typical of men of your era?

DAN: I probably did look at it that way. If you were hurting, the first thing that was said to you was "Big boys never cry" or "Men never cry." Sometimes, I think that since the times we lived through were so difficult, there wasn't opportunity for much affection. I guess there had to be affection in some families, but I'd say that most families that struggled through the Depression were too exhausted at the end of the day.

ME: How about your mother?

DAN: We certainly loved our mother, but again there was never any true affection shown. I can remember when I was 7 or 8 I was going to run away from home. I marched out the door with a shopping bag full of things and was yanked back. My mother gave me a real beating and then threw me out the door and said: "Go ahead, run away."

ME: What did you do?

DAN: I stayed out all day and at night, I went into the backyard and climbed up the pipe. I called my brother, and he opened the window and I went in. I think my parents heard me, but nothing was ever said.

ME: Back then, did you ever think that your mother behaved that way because of, or in response to, living with your father?

DAN: There is absolutely and positively no question that she had a hard life. My father was as distant from his family and my mother's family as he was from us.

ME: You mentioned earlier that your warmest memories are of the time spent with your grandmother. What made that time so special?

DAN: Not only did we get away from the city, but my grandmother was the sweetest person. Most of the time she was smiling.

ME: She was good to you and your brother?

DAN: Yes, she did things with us—she even took us out to pick apples and cherries. I shall never forget it. To me, she was a saint.

ME: You describe her as a saint, but wasn't she the mother of your father? He doesn't sound like a saint. Do you ever wonder why your dad was so distant?

DAN: I think it had to do with my grandfather. The story goes that every time Grandma got pregnant, Grandfather left home.

ME: Maybe he didn't like kids.

DAN: Apparently not. My grandmother even ran a butcher shop to support the family. She left Pittsburgh in the early 1920s with her daughter and husband, who was the dean of admissions at Penn State.

ME: We have talked about the Depression, men of your generation, your mother and father, and your ideas. Now tell me how you got along with your brother.

DAN: My brother was two years older and bigger than me. We shared the same room and bed, but we fought like cat and dog, particularly on Saturday mornings. We would always start out wrestling and the next thing I'd know we were having a fist fight. This lasted throughout most of our lives. I blame him today for the temper I have. He just teased the daylights out of me. I realize that I'm an aggressive person—I'm usually ready to fight at the drop of a hat.

ME: Did your father have a temper?

DAN: My father had a very vicious temper. Once when I was very small he picked me up and threw me against the wall. I landed on his tool chest in the kitchen.

ME: Can you think of any reason why he had such a temper?

DAN: No, no reason at all. In fact, one of his brothers, my Uncle John, seemed to care more for us and do more things around our house than father ever did.

ME: Did you get along with your Uncle John pretty well?

DAN: Very well.

ME: Let's jump into your adulthood. You stated before that you feel you are responsible for many of your behaviors. But I am curious. How do you think the way you were raised has affected you as a man?

DAN: Well, on the positive side, I think it made me very determined to do things on my own.

ME: You went on to become a very successful businessman and one of the last of a generation of men in America called self-made men. Do you think you would have accomplished these things if you hadn't come through these troubled times?

DAN: I think I would have anyway, but it made me more determined.

ME: What do you think were the negative effects of your background?

DAN: Very definitely, my drinking.

ME: Did you ever think there was a reason for your drinking?

DAN: I never stopped to analyze it. It was all around me—in my family and in business. At times I could control it by giving it up for Lent each year, but it definitely got progressively worse.

ME: I know that after many years you quit drinking and got sober. What convinced you to seek help?

DAN: My son.

ME: How?

DAN: He wrote me a letter, which I still have, which had a tremendous impact on me. Plus, my wife left me for a couple days and I went through all the horrors an alcoholic goes through. I thought I was going to die.

ME: You talk about the influence of your son and your wife, but they didn't do it; you did it.

DAN: Absolutely and positively. Someone may have all the counseling and support in the world, but if you do not have the determination, you are not going to succeed.

ME: You have been sober for seventeen years. What's different about you now as opposed to when you were drinking?

DAN: I realize the value of marriage and family, and have the ability to get up in the morning and face the day without fear.

ME: Do you have a peace about yourself today that you did not feel before?

DAN: I definitely do. I feel a lot better about myself. The only thing that still haunts me is that I can't forget my father, even now. As far as forgiving is concerned, I've gotten past the idea of forgiving or not forgiving; it's the inability to forget that bothers me.

ME: What stays with you the most about your father?

DAN: He was not truly a father in any sense of the word.

ME: So what do you think you should do with this forgiveness issue?

DAN: I believe I would like to forgive. I was told by a friend, who stabbed me in the back many times, that I was one of the most forgiving men he had ever met. I just cannot get over not being able to forgive my father. I also feel guilty about not being better to my family.

123

ME: During your drinking days, or now?

DAN: Both. But I try and I will continue to try to help the family.

ME: You have gone through so many of the issues silent sons go through, and have overcome so many of them, including alcoholism. What advice, as a man who has lived seventy years, would you offer to other silent sons, especially to younger men, about their lives?

DAN: I can't tell anyone how to live his life, but if I can help I will. There are no words of wisdom to turn a life around; there has to be a personal contact and then you go on. You know, psychiatrists see other psychiatrists. Find someone to talk to, not necessarily with the same problems, but someone you respect and who will listen to you. Keep in mind that they are willing to help you. And then *really* talk to them.

This interview was with Daniel A. Ackerman, my father.

AFTERTHOUGHTS

When I was a boy of fourteen, my father was so ignorant I could hardly stand to have the old man around. But when I got to be twenty-one, I was astonished at how much he had learned in seven years.

MARK TWAIN

Don't hate, it's too big a burden to bear.

MARTIN LUTHER KING, SR.

To become a father is not hard,
To be a father is, however.

WILHELM BUSCH

Silence propagates itself, and the longer talk has been suspended, the more difficult it is to find anything to say.

SAMUEL JOHNSON

When one has not a good father, one must create one.

FRIEDRICH NIETZSCHE

CHAPTER SEVEN

Mothers and Sons: Don't Talk about My Mother!

One of the toughest personal decisions I had to make in writing this book was whether to discuss my mother's drinking. During my boyhood her illness was our family's unspoken secret, and I carried it with me for twenty-five years before I could mention it even to friends.
GENERAL H. NORMAN SCHWARZKOPF[1]

A boy learns many unspoken rules: "Don't show pain. Don't complain if you lose. Don't tell on your friends. Pretend you are not interested in girls. Put each other down verbally, but don't punch each other out." No one ever voted on these rules. But when you were growing up, they somehow became a code to live by. And most boys carried these rules into manhood, especially the most sacred of all rules: "Say what you want about me, my father, my sister or my brother, but whatever you do, don't talk about my mother."

Talking about a boy's mom was—and still is—forbidden. On special occasions someone might mention your mother, but there were limits. If you approached the unspoken boundary, everyone got nervous. If someone said more than, "Your mother wears combat boots," it was likely to lead to combat. *You* could put your mother down, but no one else could. At least not if they wanted to keep their teeth.

Mothers and motherhood are protected by boys and men. However, many sons were not protected from their mothers. Silent sons of dysfunctional mothers were exposed to addiction, depression, prostitution, abuse, divorce, and emotional neglect. Yet their code of honor was still to protect the beloved maternal image even when what they guarded so dearly was sometimes dishonorable.

Although it is admittedly a double standard, most men believe that when a father falls from his pedestal, he is a fallen human being, but when a mother falls from hers, she is a fallen angel. A mother is held to a different set of rules, and no matter how unfair that may be, a son can't bear to see these rules broken. A silent son, like all sons, wants to preserve a positive, loving, healthy image of his mother. Facing the fall of your father may be intimidating, but facing the fall of your mother is devastating.

Perhaps we protect this image of our mothers because society is much harder on a dysfunctional mother than on a dysfunctional father. For example, if a mother has a problem with drug addiction she is considered unfit, but a father can be a lifelong alcoholic and seldom does anyone label him unfit. Boys—and even men—don't want to admit that Mom has problems. We also don't want to admit that Mom wasn't a mom. We will go to great lengths to deny this truth. In the National Adult Children of Alcoholics Research Study, I found that sons of alcoholic mothers admitted that their mothers were alcoholic at an average age of approximately 18 years old, whereas sons of alcoholic fathers admitted their fathers were alcoholic when the sons were only 12 years old.[2] Sons want so much to deny that their mother has problems that they cover it up for much longer and in turn deny themselves the help they need.

IMAGE CONSCIOUS

What is this image of a mother that we are so conscious of? What is it that we are trying to protect? Is it our image not only of a mother, but also of what we think is feminine? Robert Johnson in his book, *He: Understanding Masculine Psychology,* talks about how men maintain six different ideas of what is feminine. Three of these have to do with our mother's role and image. Johnson's types include:[3]

- *Our human mother:* our actual mother, with all her behaviors and personality characteristics, including her positive and negative patterns.
- *Our mother complex:* the part of your mother that you keep inside of you; your tendency to regress to an earlier time when she took care of you. The mother complex is your dependency on her; too much of this paralyzes you from breaking away and becoming your own man. Breaking from the mother complex is what Robert Johnson, Robert Bly, and others believe is necessary for a boy to become a man.
- *Our mother archetype:* our image of motherhood, mother, and even mother nature. The mother archetype is our positive image of femininity. It is our belief of what is nourishing, reliable, and sustaining.
- *Our fair maiden:* Each of us carries inside of us an idea of what constitutes our fair damsel. The fair maiden is our idea of the perfect woman—emotionally, spiritually, and physically. This is the one you would die for. She exists in our imagination long before we take an actual partner. We draw inspiration from her image, which gives meaning to our lives.
- *Our wife or partner:* the actual person who shares our life. This is our companion, lover, and emotional fellow traveler as we go through our lives.
- *Sophia:* the goddess of wisdom. In mythology, wisdom is feminine.

In Johnson's view, you carry all six of these elements of femininity inside you. Your first teacher of these components was your mother. What and how she taught you about being a woman influences not only what you learned and felt about *her,* but also what you learned and now feel about women in general. Even though you were a boy, it is likely that you learned what it meant to be a woman before you learned about masculinity. It is believed that very young boys and girls identify more closely with their mothers than with their fathers primarily because they spend more time with them.[4] As a result, it is not uncommon for young boys to embody more of their mother's traits than their father's. What did your mother teach you? And if she was dysfunctional, can you live with what you learned? How do you deal with admitting that your mother was dysfunctional while still maintaining a good mother image?

In my interviews, sons of dysfunctional mothers reflected this constant struggle. Their struggles with intimate relationships and not really knowing how to maintain them were at the core of many of their problems with their mothers. It is as if they just closed off their feelings about their mothers' dysfunctionality. Their struggles with their mothers were at the core of many of their problems with intimate relationships and not really knowing how to maintain them.

Not surprisingly, I found that getting silent sons to talk about their mothers was not only very difficult, but also extremely painful. Many of these sons were willing to talk about the *outcomes* of having had dysfunctional mothers, such as having problems with women today, but very few actually wanted to talk about their mothers. In the following sections I will discuss the problems common among sons of dysfunctional mothers whom I interviewed. Listed here in order of frequency, five dominant patterns prevailed: (1) the effect on their relationships with women, (2) the need to protect and defend their mothers, (3) a destroyed image of their mothers, (4) a lack of trust in women, and (5) emotional incest.

THE EFFECT ON RELATIONSHIPS WITH WOMEN

> *I don't know about others, but it seemed I could never please my mother. She yelled constantly and I learned to tune her out or stay away from home so I didn't have to hear her. As a result, I don't do well in relationships now. I like women; I just can't get along with them and I refuse to play their games.*
>
> CLIFF

The effect on their relationships with women was the number-one issue mentioned by sons of dysfunctional mothers. It is not uncommon for silent sons to have a love-hate relationship with women if their mothers were dysfunctional. Sons may react this way if their mothers sent out mixed messages which the men now, in one way or another, project onto other women in their lives. Some sons hated their mother's dysfunction but still wanted to love her. Others loved their mother but felt their mother hated them. Still others hated their mother but wanted to love other women. And finally, there were silent sons who loved the feminine image but wound up hating the women they were supposed to love. Let's look more closely at silent sons' relationships with their mothers, and their relationships with other women.

MOTHERS

If you had a dysfunctional mother, what did you learn from her? Did you learn things about her that you didn't like? Did you develop feelings about yourself that you didn't like? Did you develop attitudes and beliefs about all women that make it difficult for you to relate to women in healthy ways, or to relate to healthy women at all?

Whatever lessons you learned, it is obvious that a dysfunctional mother has a profound impact on her son. She can even make it very difficult for him to successfully separate from her as part of normal human development. Authors Robert Bly, Sam Keen, and Robert Johnson have all written about the need for a son to separate from his mother emotionally as a "rite of passage" to becoming a man. This obviously does not mean that a son no longer cares about his mother, or that he totally negates what she has taught him. Rather, it means that he has developed his own sense of self and, in turn, a healthy sense of autonomy. A healthy son can and does care deeply about his mother, but he is no longer emotionally dependent upon her.

I believe it is more difficult for a son to separate from a dysfunctional mother than from a functional mother because of the typically unpredictable behaviors of a dysfunctional mother and the mixed messages she sends out. One of the most powerful messages is that she is an especially "needy" woman. In order to be "good" and gain her approval, the son tries to meet her needs, but ironically—and unfortunately—he rarely receives the approval he seeks. The number-one problem among sons of alcoholic mothers, for example, was constantly seeking mother's affirmation and approval. This approval-

129

seeking problem was also cited by sons of dysfunctional fathers, but was ranked third.

While a son is busy seeking his mother's approval and trying to meet her many needs, she seldom manages to fulfill his. Most silent sons I spoke with believed they suffered from a lack of nurturing when it came to their mothers. Many felt that their mothers simply made them feel unwanted. They felt lonely and incapable of showing affection. As a result, these silent sons either withdrew from their mothers or tried to find nurturing elsewhere, either inside or outside of their families. Some silent sons said their siblings took responsibility for many of their mothers' duties, but could not take the place of their mothers. Were you cared for by your sister or older brother, or did you look to your father? Unfortunately, most husbands of dysfunctional wives were either physically or emotionally unavailable for their sons. Very few sons of dysfunctional fathers mentioned their mothers, but the majority of sons with dysfunctional mothers mentioned their fathers, because their fathers were usually absent.

Studies have found that 90 percent of wives of alcoholic men are likely to stay with their husbands, but only 10 percent of husbands of alcoholic wives are likely to stay. Where does this leave a son? Usually without a father, and, in most cases, with an alcoholic mother as the custodial parent. No wonder these sons felt a "nurturing deficit."

OTHER WOMEN

Obviously, there are silent sons of dysfunctional mothers who have learned to relate positively to women and who have very satisfying relationships. But many others have repeatedly told me that their mothers "set the stage" for the problems they now experience with women as adults. These men find themselves attracted to the wrong types of women and feel they never have their needs truly met in a relationship.

What kind of women are you attracted to? I don't mean physically, but emotionally. Are you attracted to women who "need" you, lean on you, but then resent your being in charge? Are you attracted to women whose problems you can solve? Or to women with poor self-esteem? What about women who eventually abandon you? If so,

130

you share some of the most common relationship problems with other sons of dysfunctional mothers.

Mothers and lovers require a man to assume two entirely separate roles. When you have negative overlap between these roles, there is trouble. Your mother is not your lover, and your lover is not supposed to be your mother. Robert Johnson, explaining his ideas of what constitutes "feminine" in the minds of all men, tells us that there is trouble when men cannot separate the two. It leads to internal confusion and poor relationships. However, it is easy to see how this can occur. Dysfunctional mothers do not project a clear and definitive image of their roles as mothers or as women. Sons of dysfunctional mothers are asked to do things that are very different from what is expected of sons of functional mothers. They then emerge with a concept of women that is not healthy, and as a result they get involved in distorted relationships.

One silent son asked me, "What is a healthy woman, anyway?" His mother was obviously not a healthy woman, and since he judged all women by the example his mother had set, he couldn't distinguish the difference. Consequently, he went around treating most women as he treated his mother. He wanted to be close to them, but did not trust them. He believed they would eventually turn against him. He entered all relationships cautiously, with the idea that they were only temporary. Like other sons of dysfunctional mothers, he did not believe he could relate honestly to women. He had little respect for them, but admitted that he needed to be around them. It is ironic that many silent sons see women as needy but are blind to their own "neediness," particularly about women.

Some silent sons I interviewed are attracted to "needy" women precisely because they think they can solve the woman's problems. What attracts them most is not the woman, but the opportunity to solve her problem and show what they can do. Either consciously or subconsciously, they are repeating a boyhood pattern that started when they tried to solve their mother's problems and were rewarded. When there were no problems to solve, there was no approval. Now, when they've solved their partners' problems, they have no reason to continue in the relationship. What is missing is not only the problems but also the assurance that they are valued.

Mothers of these silent sons seldom conveyed to their sons that they were valued.

Sons of dysfunctional mothers seldom enter into equal partnerships with women. They do not see themselves and women as equal. Are you always rescuing women who are not as competent as you, or are you convinced that you are never as competent as the women in your life? An unequal relationship happens when you think you need to take care of women, lose respect for them, project your feelings about your mother onto another woman, want to punish all women, resent women, or desperately need their approval. All of these things can keep you off balance in your relationships with women.

I noticed that many silent sons of dysfunctional mothers were angry toward women, a reaction which ultimately began with their mothers. Their relationships, no matter how well they began, usually ended in anger.

For the silent son, an unhappy ending is often interpreted not as a result of *his* anger and *his* unresolved issues about women, but rather a flaw in the woman's character. All he can say is that yet another woman has rejected and abandoned him. Mistakenly, he does not conclude that there is something wrong with his mother or with him, but rather that all women have the same thing wrong with them. He then maintains this very narrow view and keeps closing his eyes and his relationships. The silent son cannot see women differently until he successfully resolves his issues with his mother and realizes that his mother does not represent all women. Your mother is one woman in your life. She is not all women. If she is, you have unfortunately blended the six elements of the feminine into one. You will treat all women the same because you believe them all to be one and the same. And unfortunately, you are likely to end up with the same results.

PROTECT AND DEFEND

> *I developed caretaking feelings and protective feelings for my mother that women today don't want to hear about.*
>
> BRUCE

If your mother was dysfunctional while you were growing up, did you have an overly strong investment in her well-being? Did you identify with her dysfunctional behavior to the point where you began to do dysfunctional things yourself, such as getting into trouble at school, lying, or starting fistfights?

Many silent sons protected their mothers in order to help them, but also to indirectly protect themselves. This is especially true for boys who didn't want anyone speaking ill of their mother. They felt that if they could protect their mother and do things for her, she would appear normal, at least to others. Whether they realized it or not, their efforts to protect their mother, such as putting her to bed when she was drunk so that others wouldn't see her, were a way of avoiding exposure to the mother's dysfunction.

> *My problem is coping with the fact that while most sons love their mothers, they feel a sense of denial and shame when a mother is under the influence of alcohol. I had to protect her, but I felt hurt and had no one to turn to.*
>
> SID

A silent son often gauges his self-worth by how well he can protect his mother. A mother sends out strong messages to her son about his self-worth. A dysfunctional mother can let her son believe that only when he is serving her needs is he being "good." Thus, the son is trapped in the good son syndrome we mentioned earlier. The trap tightens if he also becomes convinced that he can never do enough in her eyes. She wants him to take on more and more responsibility for which he is not trained. But no matter what he does, it is never enough and she makes him feel guilty. His behavioral response is to try harder, but he can't win.

Another trap is laid for the silent son when his father either leaves his mother or is no longer emotionally involved with her. At this point the son usually hears messages to the effect that "Your father is no good, but you, son, can be good by meeting my needs." He tries to become the man his father never was.

No matter how it manifested itself, their mother's protection was an extremely heavy burden for the silent sons I spoke with. They were asked to be protectors but were not protected. The irony is that no matter how well they did or how hard they tried, they never quite succeeded.

IMAGE PROBLEMS

It is difficult to see something you value destroyed. It is even more painful when what is destroyed is a person you like or love. And when it is your own mother, you fight to prevent her from experiencing any unnecessary pain. As a son, however, you will soon realize there is little you can do about her behaviors, and the only thing left to fight for is your image of her. After a while you no longer respond to her as a person, but as a mother image.

We all want to imagine our mothers as fair and nurturing people. We want to imagine that our mother would never do anything to hurt us or other people. We want to imagine that mothers are not deviant or dysfunctional. But when the image of what a mother should be conflicts with the reality, it creates pain. I know that many silent sons are struggling with this problem. Some sons of the most incredibly dysfunctional mothers stopped themselves in our interviews and said, "I just can't talk about my mother this way." It was too painful for them to talk about the reality. It was easier to deny the dysfunction and maintain an image, even if it was false. This is how powerfully sons want to protect their mother's image. They will deny their own pain rather than admit she caused them pain.

But I also found that in the process of preserving an image, these men were growing angry. They were angry at their mothers and angry in general because the image was slipping away. No matter how hard they tried to preserve the image, their mothers continued to repeat the dysfunctional behaviors. How can you keep cleaning up after your mom and continue denying it? The answer is: You can't. Such a situation only leads to frustration, and soon frustration turns to anger. I am amazed at how many silent sons of dysfunctional mothers emerged as angry men but would not admit they were angry with their mothers. Instead, as we've already discussed, they became angry with women in general.

Robby, age 28, Ed, age 32, and Bill, age 35, grew up in an affluent family. Their father was a physician, they lived in a large house, the family was well known and respected. Their mother was an alcoholic who threw fits of rage in the house. Two of the three boys were always in trouble for fighting. Years later, two of the three brothers became alcoholic, two have been divorced twice, and all of their marriages have been violent. No one ever said anything about the mother's behavior while the boys were growing up. She never got any help, and neither did they. Their father stayed at the hospital most of the time. Robby, who sought help, states, "The most obvious problem for me was learning to recognize and accept the reality about my mother and to find ways to dump my anger.

TRUST

> *I never sensed that my mother trusted me or that we connected. She told my brother before her death that she never felt she knew what was going on with me.*
>
> RAY

The success of all relationships depends on trust. When trust is violated, a relationship is forever changed. We are raised to believe, "If you can't trust your mother, whom can you trust?" So when a son loses trust in his mother, it is as if he has lost part of himself. This has happened to many a silent son. Promises made were repeatedly broken. He could not trust her to act like a mother. He came home too often to find her passed out on the couch from drinking or drugs. He saw her with a man and she pretended it never happened. She showed no interest in his projects, friends, or feelings. She made him feel like he was supposed to be there for her, not the other way around. Eventually he felt abandoned by her. The violation of trust and the feelings of abandonment went hand in hand.

When a son learns that his mother is not trustworthy, he seldom feels worthy around her. It is not uncommon for a son to develop a sense of shame about himself and his relationship with his mother at this point. When you feel abandoned, you often perceive that you are not worth being around. You begin to doubt yourself. For a boy, the worse doubt occurs when he begins to doubt his own mother.

*A feeling of abandonment, disappointment, and shame
developed in me after I became aware of my mother's
illness.*

LEROY

Violation of trust between a mother and son also affects a son's ability to trust women later in his life. Many silent sons I interviewed entered relationships with women with a strong feeling of mistrust. After all, as far as they were concerned they had already experienced the ultimate form of betrayal when their mothers violated their trust; it was easy to transfer this onto other women. It was not just the women that these silent sons had difficulty trusting, it was also their own feelings and judgment about women. They admitted they lacked confidence in their relationships and usually expected the worst.

In many cases, the silent sons believed that they were manipulated by their mothers, and thus expected the same from other women. A typical pattern of manipulation by dysfunctional mothers is what I call "justifiable negative attention syndrome." This occurs when the mother perceives that it is only justifiable for her to receive attention from others when something terrible happens to her beyond her control—for example, she breaks a leg or has a series of illnesses. Then she gets sympathy, attention, and caring. She therefore learns to use these negative events as permissible "excuses" to justify receiving emotional support from others. The underlying problem of justifiable negative attention is a a mother's low self-esteem, which is not uncommon for a dysfunctional woman, but of course her son only sees a mother playing on his sympathy and guilt. It is not unusual for the son to reach the conclusion about his mother (and then about other women) that a woman's only path to emotional support is negative thinking. To the son, this kind of manipulation means that there is always a "game" going on with his mother. Communication is never direct. Feelings are never honest. Trust is never present.

Many silent sons admitted that they felt like they were always in a game in their relationships. The object was not to play, but to win. It never occurred to them that the true objective was to have a healthy relationship.

I fear that if I don't dominate or control women, I will be rejected, put down, or abandoned. I have a strong need for approval and affection. I need to perceive I am in charge and in control—that I am the aggressor, and that all women are unworthy of trust. Women only praise you to get something and criticize you to keep you in your place.

JEFFREY

EMOTIONAL INCEST

The fifth most common problem named by silent sons of dysfunctional mothers was "emotional incest." Emotional incest occurs when a mother shares inappropriate emotions and information with her son that should be shared with an adult. Many silent sons felt that their mothers turned them into "surrogate spouses" by transcending an invisible yet well understood boundary between mother and son.

As mentioned earlier, silent sons yearned for nurturing from their mothers but rarely received it. In cases of emotional incest, the mother appeared to give inappropriate nurturing to her son, such as when she was depressed or drinking. She would then tell her son how disappointed she was with her marriage or that she and his father hadn't slept together in years. At the same time, the mother expected her son not only to understand, but also to accept these revelations as normal exchanges between a mother and son. These disclosures only worked to distance the sons further from their mothers and, at the same time, made them feel even more ambivalence toward their mothers. Since most sons found themselves at a loss as to how to handle these situations, they often said things to their mothers that they shouldn't have in order to make their mothers feel better. While emotional incest rarely led to sexual incest, it was still abusive. Of the five areas of concern about dysfunctional mothers, this one was talked about the least.

In many cases mothers used emotional incest as a way of showing favor to their sons. The mothers would treat their sons specially or better than the other children in the family.

137

I was an only son with two sisters, and the anxiety of having to deal with being the favorite was often too much to handle. I felt sorry all the time for my younger sisters, and guilty for getting so much attention. I couldn't even tell them what she said to me.

WAYNE

As a silent son you endure these problems, like all the others, in silence. But when the source of these problems is your mother, you are forced into a protective silence. You realize that the phrase "Don't talk about my mother" applies not only to those around you, but to you as well. What do you do with the part of your mother that you carry inside you that no one must know about? What do you do with your own feelings that you have conveniently denied? If you are like most silent sons, you try to treat these feelings as if they don't matter. You dismiss them by proclaiming that you were not affected. The day comes, however, when you realize that you *were* affected and that your feelings and your reactions do matter. Maybe not to her, but to you. When that day comes you will know it. Deep feelings once buried under years of silence will emerge, and you will be faced with two choices: admitting that all of it did matter, or forever driving it all deeper inside of you.

AFTERTHOUGHTS

The supreme happiness of life is the conviction that we are loved.

VICTOR HUGO

You can always get someone to love you—even if you have to do it yourself.

TOM MASSON

A mother is a person who if she is not there when you get home from school you wouldn't know how to get your dinner, and you wouldn't feel like eating it anyway.

ANONYMOUS

MOTHERS AND SONS: DON'T TALK ABOUT MY MOTHER!

Nothing is so burdensome as a secret.

FRENCH PROVERB

Never cut what you can untie.

JOSEPH JOUBERT

CHAPTER EIGHT

Relationships: That's the Way I Am

You don't know what's wrong or even if something is wrong until someone cares enough to confront you and help you gain some insight. Once discovered, a whole new world opens up. It's such a pleasant yet somewhat bittersweet discovery.

MARK

Trouble in romantic relationships, be they heterosexual or homosexual, is the primary reason why most silent sons seek help. Regardless of the other issues they discussed, the focus of the conversation always shifted back to romantic relationships. Even when we talked about their relationships with their mothers and fathers, many times silent sons turned the discussion to the impact their dysfunctional parents had on their current relationship abilities. The problems they identified were:

- excessive caretaking behavior directed toward their partner
- need to dominate or control
- fear of intimacy
- infidelity
- lack of honesty
- inability to express emotions
- lack of communication

- anger
- fears of abandonment, getting too close, rejection, or self-disclosure
- leaving when it "gets too tough"
- low self-esteem
- fear of commitment
- inability to keep the relationship going
- mistrust
- boredom after a few years
- lack of respect for women
- inability to confide
- lack of knowledge about what a healthy relationship is
- performance anxiety

> *For me it was naiveté, just assuming relationships happened and worked because of some unknown law of nature that mandated it. Also, I think I was like some men who view compromise as a sign of weakness and thus tend to be rigid in their expectations, including role expectations in relationships.*
>
> SCOTT

These problems are common for all men. But silent sons experience relationship problems to a greater degree than men from functional families, because they bring a lot of baggage into their relationships from their pasts. This excess baggage is weighted down with pain, but the worst pain comes when they realize that their past has limited their capacity to love and be loved. So many silent sons want a healthy relationship. Many have sworn that their lives will be different from their parents'. They believe they will know love, warmth, and intimacy, only to discover that they don't know what these are, how to achieve them, or how to accept them. Do you find yourself wanting the most incredible, intense, intimate, loving relationship in the world—and then wanting to be left alone!

If you want a relationship in the worst way, that is usually how you get it. You can only be loved to the extent that you can love. Your self-esteem is correlated with how much you can love and be loved.

141

But if you are like many silent sons, low self-esteem is one of your greatest problems, especially in relationships. If your self-esteem is low, you are at a disadvantage in every relationship, and are probably not able to build a healthy one. The best prerequisite for a healthy relationship is a healthy you.

What is your definition of a healthy relationship? What is your idea of being in a relationship and doing healthy things? Have you ever been in a bad relationship? Have you ever been in a good relationship? What are the differences between the two? The following is a list of characteristics commonly found in a healthy relationship:

- You feel you are respected as a person.
- Your physical and emotional needs are met.
- You like the other person and you feel liked by them.
- You are appreciated and not taken for granted.
- You are not afraid to be yourself.
- You can communicate effectively with your partner.
- You can affirm and support one another.
- Trust is mutual and continual.
- There is a sense of humor and play.
- Responsibilities are shared.
- Privacy is respected.
- You are not constantly fighting for control.
- You both admit and seek help for your problems.
- You want to spend time together.
- Love is a verb, not a noun.
- You are both growing and the relationship is growing.
- You feel good about yourself.

How many of these statements describe your relationship? If any of these characteristics are lacking in your relationship, you know you are in trouble and so is your relationship. Too often I listened to silent sons who did not have these characteristics in their relationships, but settled for less because they did not think much of themselves.

MEN AND RELATIONSHIPS

When men talked about their relationships with me they often ended the interview by shrugging, pausing, and stating "That's the way I am." This phrase was used so frequently and universally by sons of both functional and dysfunctional parents that I started to suspect they all knew each other. After a while I began to realize that the statement "That's the way I am" had many connotations. Just as many men admitted to having difficulty expressing themselves in relationships, they also had difficulty understanding themselves. And they dismissed their confusion with a simple statement. For many men "That's the way I am" meant "Take it or leave it." Others meant, "I would like to change, but I don't know any other way." Still others meant, "I feel trapped in the way I am." Regardless of the hidden meaning, however, they were the way they were because they were men. There are things about men and women that are unique to each. Too often, rather than appreciating these differences we condemn or blame each other for being different. Does that mean we want the other to be like us? If push comes to shove, do men really want women to be like men? Do women really want men to be like women? I doubt it. So why, when we don't understand each other, do we criticize what we don't know? Love can be limited in many ways, but the limitation is likely to begin with not understanding ourselves and others.

Does this mean that because we are men we are limited in our capacity to form healthy relationships? Obviously, those of us who have trouble in our relationships must think so. Healthy men do not. Healthy men are not limited either in their capacity to form relationships or in their capacity to love.

The word "love" is both overused and underused by men. Do you say "I love my car"? "I love to golf"? "I love hunting"? "I love music?" The beach? These tools? But the question is, Do you love people?

We use the word "love" so loosely, but have difficulty with it when it counts. We use it to refer to objects and things that are distant, but have trouble when it comes to people who are close. We debate and contemplate the meaning of love, but we often have a very limited

143

definition of love which makes us limited lovers. Which of the following fits your definition of a lover: one who loves 500 different partners once, or one who loves one partner 500 times?

As men, our capacity to love is not limited by simply being male. If it is limited it is because we have learned limitations, not because we are less capable of loving than women are. The key is not our capacity to love but our ability to express it. How do we usually express love? In his book *Male Intimacy,* Michael McGill points out five common ways men show love and share with others: sex, giving, touch, intellectualizing, and listening.[1] These five ways can also be used to withhold love in relationships.

SEX

> *Lord, make me chaste—but not yet.*
> ST. AUGUSTINE

Sex, intimacy, love, and emotions are confusing. Men can have sex without intimacy. Men can have intimacy without sex. Or men can have both. If you ask men what they want in their relationships, many will say "more sex." However, this does not mean they don't want intimacy. In fact, many men believe that sex *is* intimacy. This is a significant issue of debate in many relationships. Many men think that if you are going to be intimate you have sex, while women believe you can be intimate without sex. Many men who have relationship problems are limited in their ways of sharing or being intimate. How many ways do you know to be intimate that are not sexual? How well do you communicate in your relationships? Can you communicate with more than your organ? Sex is important, but if sex is the only thing you have then you only have a sexual relationship. In order to have sex some men need a reason, while others only need a place. Which do you need?

GIVING

A gift is a way of sharing ourselves, but it shouldn't be a substitute for giving ourselves. Do you mostly give material possessions, or a part of yourself?

Often when we don't know how to express ourselves, we do it with gifts. Giving is a wonderful gesture, but you must also consider your motivation when giving a gift. A man and woman may see another man walking down the street carrying flowers. While the woman may think, Oh, isn't that sweet, the man sees the flowers and thinks, Boy, did he screw up!

Have you ever given a "guilt" gift? When you do this, are you not hoping that somehow the gift will convey more than you can or are willing to say? When you do this, is it because you would rather spend $500 than express your emotions? Do you give *in addition* to show-ing your love, or *in lieu* of showing your love?

Some men give to a fault. They believe that their partners will accept their gifts as a sign of love, but some men's gifts are just substitutes for affection. They know that they have been physically or emotionally absent and hope that the gift makes up for it. Still other men give because they love their partners so much they feel they cannot do enough. But there can be no real appreciation when the receiver would rather have the giver than the gift. After all, how much meaning does a diamond or ring have when it is on a hand that isn't being held?

TOUCH

Touching someone is a powerful expression. When you are trying to communicate or express yourself and you fail, touching can become your last and most powerful resort. When a friend is in agony and you don't know what to say, your hand on his shoulder says it all. When you can't find the right words, the right touch says, "I'm here."

Men are very conscious of the power of touch, but we are also afraid to use it too much. We hesitate to touch another man beyond a handshake, to hug a boy after he reaches a certain age, or to touch a woman in a platonic way. In our relationships we often use touch not only as a means of expression, but also as the testing ground for how close we can get. Touching is one of the most confusing ways of sharing for men, and, like all facets of a relationship it requires bal-ance. On the one hand, touching conveys a very powerful message, while on the other it can be easily misconstrued.

Intellectualizing

Disclosure is important for intimacy and for a healthy relationship. When one partner believes that he or she is totally open about his or her feelings but the other partner is not, the relationship is often in trouble. Note that in this context disclosure means more than talking. The intellectualizer talks about everything *but* his feelings.

Intellectualizing can occur in several forms, but the one most common to men is focusing on logic and rationality. Consider this scenario: Your female partner brings up a problem in your relationship, and expresses herself very emotionally. In response, do you say, "OK, let's look at this rationally"? or "You're not being logical"? I guarantee you, these words will get you into further trouble. When she wants to deal with problems emotionally and you want to deal with them logically, you are sending her many messages. You are telling her that she is being illogical, irrational, and unreasonable. You are telling her that her feelings are not legitimate and that her emotional approach is wrong. She is bound to think you are not considering her feelings and to become even more emotional about it.

What do you do when someone reacts emotionally to a problem and tells you about it? Do you listen and then intellectualize? Ironically, when you do this you are not processing what is happening. Intellectualizing keeps you in your head and out of your heart. The next time an issue comes up in your relationship, don't jump to intellectualize—be spontaneous, and tell your partner what you're *feeling* right from your heart.

Listening

We all want to be listened to, but we are not all good listeners. If you can do both in your relationship, you have a good one.

Some men have a difficult time listening to anything. Ironically, these same men want, and often demand, to be listened to themselves. When you don't listen you are telling your partner that he or she is not important. When you do listen, you communicate respect. Respect is a must for a healthy relationship.

RELATIONSHIPS: THAT'S THE WAY I AM

I met a young man several years ago in Washington, D.C., who knew a lot about listening and respect. I was speaking at a national Children of Alcoholics conference, and after I finished he came up and began talking with me. He worked in a mental health agency, and wasn't sure he was qualified to help people but admitted he was trying his best. Before we departed I asked him if he had a business card. After all, this is a very common practice—as professionals, we all have our cards that list our titles, addresses, phone numbers, and other important information to let people know who we are and how to find us. We exchanged cards. On his were two words: his name, Michael, and under his name the word "listener." He was qualified.

If you are a good listener, people are attracted to you because you ask questions, want to know all about them, and make them feel important. But are you the type of good listener who will not disclose information about yourself? There is a reciprocal side to listening, and that is talking—or, more specifically, sharing yourself.

In order to be loving, you may need to break with the traditional stereotypical ideas about how you *should* act in your relationships. A good relationship requires you to take risks, but up to now you may have settled for being safe. What do you do when trouble occurs in your relationship? Do you immediately head for the emotional middle of the road, where you don't have to express yourself? Do you shut down in conflict, withdraw from your partner, and keep your feelings to yourself? These behaviors do nothing but limit our abilities to be healthy in our relationships.

You may know men who are great in relationships. What can you learn from them? I am not talking about the great studs, but rather the men who know how to keep healthy relationships alive and growing. Usually these men know one common fact about quality relationships: They require work and they require two people to get it done.

COMMON RELATIONSHIP PROBLEMS FOR SILENT SONS

Besides the issues all men in relationships face, what special problems confront silent sons? While our problems are probably not so different

147

from those of men from normal families, they are inevitably compounded by our past.

If you are a silent son who has low self-esteem and is carrying a lot of old emotional baggage, you are at high risk for developing negative relationships. Looking for a relationship to replace pain usually means you bring pain into the relationship. When all you desperately want is for someone to understand your pain, pain is usually all you have to give.

No relationship can make up for a lost or troubled childhood. A relationship is not a place for therapy. If you want a therapeutic relationship, contact a counselor. A romantic relationship is for adults who want intimacy and want to grow. Growing means you must examine your concerns and be willing to invest some hard work in finding solutions to the problems you identify. Read the section below to see how your concerns compare with those of the silent sons I surveyed. Silent sons shared five common concerns about relationships: (1) inability to express emotions, (2) fear of intimacy, (3) inability to trust, (4) fear of inadequacy and rejection, and (5) need to control relationships.

INABILITY TO EXPRESS EMOTIONS

I was speaking to a large group about men and women from dysfunctional families. The audience was very quiet. I started talking about relationships and my idea that men's roles were changing. The silence was suddenly broken by a woman who shouted, "Show us." The women began applauding. The men said nothing, but I'd bet most were thinking, We will, we will, as soon as we figure out how.

The inability to express emotion is the most common relationship problem among silent sons. Most of us truly feel that we are emotional, we just have difficulty showing our feelings for a variety of reasons. Most silent sons probably didn't see much affection or other displays of emotion from their fathers, and what was seen was probably negative. By example, we learned that it is okay to express negative emotions such as anger or frustration, but not positive ones such as love, warmth, or caring.

Do you find yourself frequently complaining but seldom praising?

Is it difficult for you to express positive emotions? Do you sometimes feel that showing love, appreciation, or tenderness leaves you feeling hollow or empty? It takes a healthy person to express positive emotions, and it is very difficult to maintain a healthy relationship when either you or your partner don't truly like yourself. Healthy relationships are grounded on the expression and exchange of negative and positive emotions, but there's got to be a balance.

Naturally, a silent son's inability to express himself clearly causes communication problems. Sometimes we fail to communicate because we hold ourselves back even when we want to be more involved. Our partners often sense this and ask, "Why didn't you say something?" or "Why don't you tell me these things?" Do you usually just shrug or mutter that you didn't want to be a bother when inside you're thinking, I was going to tell you—when I got around to it? The next time you're about to hold back, ask yourself, What am I waiting for—permission to speak? Holding back means you don't want to take the risk of revealing who you are and what you think, feel, or believe.

Childhood role models play a large part in conditioning you to seek the safety of the emotional middle. If you are like many silent sons who emerged from dysfunctional families, you grew up thinking minimal communication in a relationship was the norm. Based upon what you witnessed, you may also believe that if you have a problem you can tell your best friend but not your spouse. You may not mean to, but you are subconsciously restricting the communication within your relationship. You don't need to tell your partner everything—I think men should keep some things to themselves. But things that are important to your relationship should be shared. When you can say things to others that you can't say to your partner, communication has become limited. A relationship can only grow so far within the bounds of limited communication.

The famous author and lecturer Leo Buscaglia tells a story about a man whose wife always wanted a red dress.[2] The man knew she wanted it because she told him she did, but he never bought one for her. When the man's wife died, he asked Leo if he thought it would be all right to bury his wife in a red dress. When Leo tells this story he always asks his audience, "What are you waiting for?" If you have something to do, to say, to share, do it. You don't have forever. The time is now.

As a silent son, you have much to give but have waited too long to release your feelings. If you love her, tell her. If your life would be empty without her, tell her. Put this book down. Go find her right now. Call her if you have to and say, "I just wanted to tell you I love you, I'm glad you're in my life."

Few of us like to be told, "You don't know how to communicate." You may feel you open up and share things, but if you are experiencing communication problems maybe you are not completely open or are not sharing enough. Most communication problems indicate that there is both too little talking and too little listening, leaving one or both partners feeling cheated.

FEAR OF INTIMACY

Intimacy is emotional bonding, and true intimacy begins with liking yourself. It is unrealistic to expect someone else to like and love you when you don't like what you are offering. Think about it. Would you like to live with you? If your answer is yes, you probably feel good about yourself. If your answer is no, you are likely to be keeping things inside you that you are afraid to show. Intimacy means showing yourself to another person. You can only do this when you like what you are about to expose and do not fear rejection.

Most research about intimacy indicates that women are much more aware and sensitive about what is intimate in a relationship. Michael McGill believes that intimacy is what makes us close to each other. He breaks down the process of being intimate into the following five elements.[3]

Time Together

We become intimate with other people when we are physically close to them and share experiences with them over an extended period of time. We need to be able to build on these experiences to further our relationships. If you can only relate to a given person in the specific context in which you once spent time together, your relationship is frozen in time. When you see an old high school friend, do you talk only about what you did in high school, or can you build on that friendship by talking about what you are doing now? If not, you are not able to transcend your old time together and to use it as a foundation for further sharing. Intimacy is built over time, but it is shared in the present.

Breadth of Interpersonal Exchange

Becoming intimate means sharing many things. Many of us think we have friends because we do things with them, but how much of ourselves do we actually share? You might have one friend for golf, one for the movies, one for talking business, and another for just hanging around. All of these people know a little about you. Intimacy means one person knows a lot about you—the "real" you, not just the you you offer to the public. In an intimate relationship a wealth of things are shared: feelings, thoughts, and fears, as well as fun activities. Relationships that revolve around common interests have little to sustain them over time.

Depth of Personal Exchange

Intimacy means you exchange personally valued information. You share things that are important to you. Many silent sons admit that their partners tell them, "I don't really know you, you don't tell me anything meaningful." Silent sons rarely share their deepest feelings and rarely experience this kind of intimacy.

Exclusivity

Intimacy occurs between two people when they realize that what they have cannot be duplicated with another person. Intimacy is the property of your relationship, and you can easily withhold it by remaining afraid of commitment to exclusivity.

Is there someone in your life who knows you better than anyone else? Good. That means the two of you share something special. Your relationship might be built on an intense experience that you survived together, a great time you spent together, or simply just growing together. Exclusivity creates an element in a relationship that is hard to measure, but has immense impact. You're able to read each other like a book because you each know the meaning of the other's pages.

"We"

If a relationship is intimate, there are three participants coming together: I, you, and we. A feeling of "we" means you possess not only individual but also collective concerns about who you are. Relationships that fall apart usually lose the "we" concern first. A relationship of two people who put their own individual interests first all the time is not a "we" relationship, and ultimately not an intimate one.

INABILITY TO TRUST

Relationships need expression and thrive on intimacy, but they are built on trust. For the silent sons I interviewed, trust problems occurred in two primary areas of their relationships: they didn't believe they could trust their own judgment, and they didn't believe they could completely trust their partner. Silent sons can find it very difficult to trust others, especially in an intimate context where deep hurt is always possible. There are no guarantees even in the healthiest of relationships. You can invest everything and the relationship might still not remain intact. There are great rewards in relationships, but there are also risks. Trust requires risks. Some silent sons of alcoholic mothers have openly admitted they do not trust women. They have had their trust violated as boys and they know the pain of betrayal.

How much do you trust the person you are in a relationship with? Do you trust her or him with information about yourself, or do you protect yourself by not revealing too much? Intimacy and trust belong together; it is incredibly difficult to have one and not the other. Do you find that you open yourself up more to strangers than to people with whom you are supposedly intimate? What does this tell you? You want your partner to be trustworthy, but trust her with little information. You long for intimacy but don't realize that it is *your* inability to trust that prevents it from happening.

Your partner knows it when you don't totally trust her. She can sense your holding back and feels resentful. She trusts you, but you can't reciprocate, so she feels she is being treated unfairly. On the other hand, she may feel that your lack of trust in her means you yourself are not trustworthy. How much can *you* be trusted in a relationship? Can your partner depend on you, or does your fidelity fluctuate with your fear of betrayal? In a healthy relationship trust needs to be constant. You need to know, and so does your partner, that you can be yourself and the relationship will not only endure but deepen. When trust disappears, so does the relationship.

How do you learn to trust someone? You can begin by taking small risks and using your head. If you are the type of silent son who always holds back, don't let it go all at once. You will be uncomfortable and likely to get hurt. Use discretion. You need to know something about whom you are trusting. In order for trust to develop, you need to be around trustworthy people. If you keep getting burned, maybe you need to quit dating flamethrowers. Try dating healthier people. If you are already in a relationship but keep holding back, start establishing trust by taking small risks. Start by sharing things about yourself. Your partner has probably been waiting a long time for this to happen. Trust needs to be built over time—it doesn't just happen overnight.

FEAR OF INADEQUACY AND REJECTION

As men we might eventually admit to a lot of things, but admitting to fear will probably be the last of them. Nevertheless, I have heard a lot of silent sons talking about their fears whether they knew it or not. Some talked about their fear of abandonment. They admitted they had difficulty expressing themselves, trusting, and being intimate, but what they feared most was that their partners would leave. Do you have fears about getting too close to someone? If so, it is possible that what you fear is not intimacy but losing control over yourself to someone. Many silent sons share this fear. They think they will suddenly become weak and vulnerable if they admit to needing somebody.

> *I don't know if it's related, but my pattern in relation-ships is to cut and run when it gets difficult, or when somebody gets too close.*
>
> WARD

153

Our fears are often associated with feeling vulnerable. Men don't like being vulnerable; we were taught to stand on our own two feet, and our fears sometimes create a constant struggle between what we think is masculine and what constitutes a healthy relationship.

Many silent sons are also afraid of not finding a healthy relationship or, if we're lucky enough to find one, of spoiling it because we're not healthy enough to maintain it.

Many silent sons settle for less because they think they're not entitled to a good relationship because of their problems or fears. Healthy relationships are not made by people who are fearless. No way. Healthy relationships are made by people who refuse to let their fear stand in the way. They know that there are no guarantees, but they also know that if you live in fear there are no possibilities for happiness.

You can always get a guarantee for trouble, but a healthy relationship requires you to take chances. Remember your first high school dance? You stood with the other guys staring at a special girl you had wanted to ask to dance for weeks or months. What held you back? Fear. Fear that if she said no you would feel rejected. Fear of what the other guys would say when you walked back, humiliated. Somehow you learned that your fear was never as great as the sheer exultation that you felt when she said yes. Marching through your fear on that gymnasium floor is the same task you tackle every time you take a risk in your relationship. You have to take hold of your fear before it takes hold of you. You may still be in the corner in the gym. You may have danced and danced, maybe with the same partner for years, maybe with many partners. But if you are still standing in the corner, it is time to ask your partner to dance, just like you asked that girl in the gym.

NEED TO CONTROL

I have either tried to control whatever woman I am with, having to know at all times where she is, what she's doing, and who she's doing it with, or I have completely released my power, letting her say or do whatever she wanted to me just as long as she didn't leave me. I have

*at times been more in touch with her feelings than my
own. Hypervigilance, fear of abandonment, and jeal-
ousy have troubled me in relationships both before and
after recovery.*

JACK

Do you always need to be in control to feel comfortable in a
relationship? Does your partner resent that you dominate the decision
making? Would you rather be in control of a poor relationship or have
shared responsibility in a healthy one?

Control problems are not easy to break. As men we have been
taught to think we "should" be in charge. And for most silent sons,
taking control has been a means of survival. But such an attitude can
ruin a healthy relationship. Your partner develops resentment when
she sees you more as a parent than as a partner. Control means you
dominate the relationship—physically, psychologically, economi-
cally, or emotionally—in order to meet your needs, because you don't
know how else to do it. When you control a relationship you expose
your self-doubt about your capacity to be healthy.

Are you a controlling partner? Have you ever thought that your
partner might resent many of your behaviors, but you have intimidated her so much that she is afraid to speak up? Do you assume her
silence is compliance? Have you ever considered it might be fear?
There is nothing worse than living with a person you fear. Problems
crop up, but you don't understand why. Your partner approaches you
cautiously because you have taught her that she must deal with you
delicately and indirectly. When you are a controlling person, your
partner attempts to become a counter-controller in order to survive.
You probably don't notice your own controlling behavior, but when
you notice hers you accuse her of wanting to control everything.
Answer the following questions to determine how much you control
your partner.

1. When there is a problem in your relationship, do you blame
   your partner?
2. Do you sometimes drink too much and become physically or
   verbally abusive?

155

3. Does your partner suspect that you have been involved with other people?

4. Are you usually late, or do you stand up your partner for appointments or dates?

5. Do you forbid, or criticize your partner's partaking in outside activities?

6. Do you embarrass your partner in front of other people?

7. Do you get angry when your partner disagrees with you?

8. Do you accuse your partner of flirting when you know he or she is not?

9. Do you ever follow your partner to check up on her or him?

10. Do you criticize the way your partner looks or dresses?

11. Do you insist on driving the car all the time?

12. Have you ever hit your partner?

13. Do you do or say things to your partner that your partner never thought she or he would hear from you?

14. Do you stop talking or withdraw your affection when you want to win an argument or make a point?

15. Do you tell your partner you need your "freedom" or "space"?

16. Have you pushed your partner or used some other physical act to make your partner comply?

17. Do you not allow your partner to have a checking account and do you give her or him an allowance to pay the bills?

18. Do you use sex to quiet your relationship doubts?

19. Do you typically not show any interest in your partner's day?

20. Do you give your partner extra money or buy your partner presents when he or she has been "good"?

21. Do you call your partner a nag or accuse your partner of stirring up trouble if he or she wants to talk about problems in your relationship?

22. Do you usually call your partner by a demeaning or derogatory nickname?

23. Do you usually not phone when you're going to be late?

24. Do you want your partner around when you are home?

25. Have you ever been arrested?

26. Do you feel angry or uncomfortable when your partner gets attention?
27. Do you put down your partner's accomplishments?
28. Do you trivialize or make fun of your partner's feelings?
29. Does your partner often say you are too critical?
30. Do you ever flirt with someone else in front of your partner?
31. Do you ever make your partner feel sorry for you?
32. Do you ever frighten your partner with threats?
33. Do you find fault with your partner's friends and people close to them?

If you answered yes to twenty or more of these questions, you are a very controlling partner. If you answered yes to twelve or more, you are quite controlling. If you answered yes to five or more, you are somewhat controlling.[4]

If your relationship is out of balance, you might be able to get it back by giving up some of your control. Giving up control does not mean letting the other person walk all over you. It doesn't mean becoming a wimp. It means you feel good enough about yourself to be in a relationship without having to manipulate the other person. You have a choice: Hold on to control or hold on to your relationship.

AFTERTHOUGHTS

You will find as you look back upon your life that the moments when you have really lived are the moments when you have done things in the spirit of love.
HENRY DRUMMOND

Respect is love in plain clothes.
FRANKIE BYRNE

A man is only as good as what he loves.
SAUL BELLOW

He disliked emotion, not because he felt lightly, but because he felt deeply.

John Buchan

If you want to be loved, be lovable.

Ovid

CHAPTER NINE

"Are You Listening to Me?" What Women Say about Us

This chapter is about the women in our lives and what they want us to hear. These women can be our mothers, sisters, wives, or lovers. They love us, recognize our wounds, and often see our pain before we do. It is difficult for them to stand by and watch us in agony. By communicating their concerns to us, they are trying to reach us and get us to take a good look at ourselves.

What do these women want us to hear? I have interviewed over 100 women who are or were in some type of relationship with silent sons. They are telling us what our silence means to them—even if we don't know what it means to us. You don't have to debate, argue, agree, defend yourself, or nod your head. All you have to do is listen.

Do any of these statements sound familiar?

- I can't reach him.
- He doesn't talk much.
- He's good to others, but doesn't take care of himself.
- I'm trying to understand him, but I'm lost.
- He uses infidelity to sabotage intimacy.
- He doesn't want to commit.

- He has to be the best at whatever he does.
- He lacks communication skills for ordinary situations.
- He withdraws when he is frustrated or hurt.
- He is afraid to take risks.
- He doesn't want to be dependent.
- How do I get him to open up?
- He can't feel his own pain or anyone else's.
- He wants a perfect relationship without changing.
- He's responsible at work but irresponsible at home.
- No tears, no fears—he's a rock.

These are a few of the statements I heard from wives, lovers, mothers, and sisters of silent sons. Regardless of what they specifically said, all of these women are worried about us. And as much as we may like to, we can't discount their comments as simply women talking about men. There is much more to it. Most of these women in our lives are trying to reach us but don't know how. They see our pain but they also see our potential. Admittedly, some of them think we are too stubborn to change or we are incapable of maintaining a healthy relationship, and are waiting for us to grow up. However, these women are the minority. Most want to help, but the women I interviewed told me it was hard for them to help us because of the following problems: (1) We won't let them in, (2) we do too much caretaking, (3) we can't commit, (4) we project our problems onto others, (5) we fail to take care of ourselves.

LET ME IN

> My five sons are silent sons. All of them are college graduates, have good positions, and work hard. They enjoy sports and have their own lives. But I don't know who they really are or what they're about. I have no idea of what they think about how they grew up or about me as a parent. I have written many healing letters to each of them, but have never received a response.
>
> MARLENE

All women do not see all silent sons the same. But regardless of our personalities or differing behaviors, the "Let me in" theme was strong. It was as if they were saying, "I know him, but I don't."

Is this true for you? Do you let a woman get to know you to a point, and then close the door emotionally? Do you find yourself restricting her access to you? The women in our lives are trying to tell us that when we let them in they feel close to us and see this as intimacy. When we don't, they feel rejected.

> *There is no communication and no vulnerability in our relationship. Sex is viewed as intimacy and it is short and mechanical. I bring up an issue and he says it doesn't exist.*
>
> GLORIA

When you tell a woman in one way or another, "Take me or leave me, but don't expect to get to know me," you give her little choice. Many times, after repeated attempts, she will leave. You may then ask yourself, What did I do? The answer is, Nothing—but that's precisely the problem. If she is going to share your life that is exactly what she wants to do: share. And that means share all of it. But if you are like many men, you only want to share the good things. When you are frustrated or angry you withdraw. You can withdraw by becoming distant, changing the subject, telling her she won't understand, or telling her nothing is wrong, when she can plainly see that something *is*. All of these symptoms are telltale signs that you have become emotionally distant. If a woman tries to close the gap, you only move farther away.

> *The greatest problem I see as a mother is my son's inability to share his feelings. He's closed. He operates as though he's on the outside.*
>
> GRACE

People can only get as close as we let them. Many of the women in our lives are telling us that they want to be close to us. They are telling us that we are good men with good qualities. They want a quality relationship with us, but a quality relationship requires two participants who are equally involved.

When you were a boy, did you ever have a friend who always played at your house but never invited you over to his? His toys were always off-limits, he never brought anything to play with, and all he wanted to do was stay at your house and use your things. Such a friendship seldom lasted. You felt used or just lost interest. You felt he didn't play fair. Likewise, the women in our lives want us to play fair. When you withhold yourself from the woman in your life, you are like the boy who never shared his toys. Such a relationship seldom lasts.

TOO MUCH CARETAKING

> *He is the biggest caretaker in the world, never letting me do anything alone or for myself. It drives me crazy! I tell him when he's doing it and to leave me alone, and he says, "OK, I'm sorry." But then he does it again five minutes later. I told him I didn't want a relationship with him anymore because of this, and now he's trying to take me as a hostage.*
>
> WILMA

Do you ever feel like you're being blamed for doing exactly what you think you should do? Many silent sons see their role as a partner and as a man defined by taking care of women, but most women find this overwhelming. They don't want a caretaker—they want a friend and a lover.

Even when your intentions are only good, excessive caretaking can send a woman the wrong messages. It can tell her that you don't think she can take care of herself. It can tell her you don't trust her. It can tell her you are more interested in taking care of her than actually *being* with her. These messages are not healthy for any relationship.

As silent sons we may have witnessed our fathers neglecting our mothers, so some of us vowed that we would always be there for the woman in our lives. We promised ourselves we would be the best provider and caretaker possible. But there is such a thing as overkill, and it results in women feeling smothered and us feeling rejected. It also leaves us wondering: I do everything for her; what does she want, anyway? She wants equality. She wants to be a partner, not a child.

Excessive caretaking behavior can tell us several important things about ourselves. It tells us we have a narrow definition of our role in a relationship. It tells us we have an unhealthy need for control. More importantly, it tells us we are good at giving, even to a fault, but we are not good at receiving.

Is it hard for you to let her do something for you? I'm not talking about making dinner. I'm talking about letting her do something meaningful and being able to accept it. For example, she wants to plan your vacation and keep the destination a surprise. Would you let her? Can you thank her for doing something that you usually do, or do you tell her that next time she should leave it alone?

You can keep a person at a distance by always insisting on being in charge. And the more you insist, the more she'll back off. When a woman feels overwhelmed in a relationship, the first thing she wants to do is take time out. The caretaker seldom understands this, tries to do more, and ends up adding fuel to the fire.

> *I felt trapped, resentful, and scared. I wished he would stop, but I couldn't tell him. He picked up on these feelings and began demanding even more. His "I love you" wasn't an offer, which he now admits; it was a demand. He wanted to control everything.*
>
> LOUISE

The caretaker is a demanding man. He demands that his woman be dependent on him and that he be in charge of everything. He conveys that only he can give and she can only receive. He might even believe that if he doesn't do everything for her she will leave. His caretaking behavior then is motivated by fear of abandonment. However, if this is true he probably also feels used. Either way, this is not a healthy motivation for a relationship. Even if he is very subtle in his caretaking, it will eventually cause him trouble. To avoid or overcome this problem he needs to be *more involved* and *less in charge*.

CAN'T COMMIT

> *Before me, he ran away from someone he could have*
> *had an intimate relationship with. Then he stayed with*
> *someone he had no intention of committing to. Now he*
> *is living with me and after six months I became comfort-*
> *able enough to speak my heart. Immediately, he started*
> *picking fights over little things. I guess he's getting ready*
> *to go.*
>
> CONNIE

Do you like to play it safe in your relationships? Do you hold a little back and not play all your cards? If so, you've probably been asked if you are afraid of commitment. Fear of commitment is strong for many silent sons. If this is true for you, you may have watched other relationships fall apart or witnessed it happen in your own family. As a result you probably don't trust women, have a low opinion of marriage, or fear getting hurt. You may think that if you don't commit you won't get hurt. But your partner may be telling you that if you don't commit you won't have a relationship.

Women want commitment in their relationships, men want safety, and we never think that these could be the same thing. It seems the common complaint from many women is that they want balance in their relationships and we aren't giving it. We hold back, take charge, give too much, don't commit, or are limited in our expression of intimacy. Often on the negative side of the scale, we rarely meet them in the middle.

> *I can't get through his wall of defense. There is no reci-*
> *procity in his willingness to connect. He is either giving*
> *too much or taking too much. There's no balance.*
>
> IVA

According to the women I interviewed, the worst kind of relationship imbalance occurs when men want total commitment from women but won't reciprocate. Were you ever involved in a work project with another person which called for an equal sharing of responsibilities? If you did more than your share, did you feel you were being taken advantage of or cheated? This is how your partner feels about you when you ask for what you will not give. Commitment is a pledge to exchange emotions and responsibility in a relationship. Without commitment, your partner can't rely on you. If a crisis occurs, she fears you will run and you probably would. But ask yourself: What are you running from—the crisis? her? or your unwillingness to commit?

The women I interviewed felt that our inability to commit, even when we wanted to, is the result of impeded emotions—that is, we don't know how to accurately express ourselves and our emotions to our partners. And we can't commit what we can't express.

> *He doesn't know what he feels. He's reluctant to grow.*
> *He would rather play, he says, than learn how to relate.*
> *He does relate sometimes, though, as long as I don't*
> *interfere. Commitment! He panics if something looks like*
> *it will go on "forever."*
>
> ALLISON

PROJECTION

> *My mother-in-law! She was a martyr and didn't want*
> *him to treat me better than her. She didn't want to give*
> *up complete control of her children's lives. He refused to*
> *make decisions or be responsible because his mother*
> *always did it for him.*
>
> RANDI

Many women echoed the feeling that we take unresolved issues with one woman and project them on another. Many women felt that silent sons were trying to resolve past issues with their mothers in their current love relationships.

165

He saw his mother as a saint, and he divided women into two groups: saints were the kind you marry, and whores were the ones you played with. He was incredibly confused about his own maleness and how he was supposed to express it. He often witnessed his father getting drunk and abusive, so he became his mother's protector. He never saw a man express feelings appropriately and he was terrified of being like his dad. He simply went through life fearful of feeling anything.

MARTHA

The woman in your life does not represent all women. She wants to be treated for who she is to you, not for what other women did to you. But the message that she often receives is that you are using her to resolve your past issues. To understand this, imagine you are dating a woman who recently broke up with someone else. Your conversations are naturally dominated by talking about her past relationship. Since you are on date behavior, for the first couple of dates you listen and try to be understanding. After a while you get sick of hearing about the other guy, and if it continues you want out, right? This is exactly how a woman feels when it seems you are using her not only to resolve your past issues with other women, but also to work through your other problems.

Another classic example of projection involves denying your problems and attributing them to someone else. Do you deny that you are controlling, but blame your wife for being controlling? Maybe you deny that you can't get close, but describe her as very distant. You have problems, but since you project them onto her, you expect her to solve them. When she can't, you blame her.

NOT TAKING CARE OF OURSELVES

I have five brothers and one father. All sons of alcoholics, all alcoholic, all in denial, and all in a great deal of pain, but ashamed to cry or deal with their pain constructively.

ROSETTA

Women noticed that silent sons seldom do a very good job of taking care of themselves. They said this was especially true of men who do too much for others, are driven occupationally, have tendencies toward perfectionism or addictions, have stress-related disorders, and have an overly developed sense of responsibility.

Have you been told by a woman to take care of yourself? Have you been told she is worried that you are run-down, or that you should slow down? If so, have you listened to her? If you are like most silent sons, you fit the old Timex watch ad slogan: "Takes a licking and keeps on ticking."

Why don't we take care of ourselves? Don't we think we are worth it? Or is this just "typical" male behavior? Taking care of ourselves is not limited to seeking medical attention when we are sick. It also means caring for ourselves emotionally and spiritually. Most of us think we are too busy to care for ourselves, yet we find time to care for the car, the lawnmower, and the kids' bicycles.

> Some are extremely sensitive and tender to others, but not to themselves.
>
> VAL

Many women said they got tired of caring more for our well-being than we did, especially when it came to our emotional well-being. Do you only show a woman your emotional side when it needs repair? Some women will identify with you when you are in pain because that is the only time you let them in. But after a while, they begin to feel used and will probably resent it. A healthy partner wants to be involved with all of you, not just your down side. If she helps you when you are down, it is to bring you back up. You may know men who have ended a relationship with a woman because she physically "doesn't take care of herself." If you don't take care of yourself emotionally, are you any different than the undesirable woman who "let herself go"?

167

BALANCE IN RELATIONSHIP SKILLS

*If they can get through the pain of who they think they
are and see who they really are, they become really
special people and a joy to be with.*

TRACY

Women want us to be more consistent in our behavior toward
them. They also want us to explore all our feelings before we turn to
anger. Do you blow up first and *then* sort out your feelings? When you
are in a relationship, do your moods and behaviors run hot and cold?
Do you find yourself at first totally involved and then withdrawing
into solitude? Do you act one way when you feel another? She can see
right through it. If she is going to bother spending time with you to
establish a relationship, you can bet she would prefer to be with the
real you. The last thing she wants to relate to is a façade while the real
you hides inside.

The same is true of sex. She wants her sex to be a balance of
intimacy and love. If the real you hides inside, there is no intimacy in
sex and she knows it.

Intimacy is communication. A relationship without it is completely
imbalanced. If she gives herself to you physically and emotionally, she
is giving completely. And she wants the same from you. Have you
ever liked someone more than they liked you? How did it make you
feel? Weren't you hoping that eventually she would like you as much
as you liked her? You were looking for reciprocity. You were looking
for balance. You wanted to like and be liked equally.

Balance in a relationship begins with each person. As individuals,
we must feel good about ourselves. We must have an internal sense
of balance. For many silent sons this is difficult. We have kept things
to ourselves for so long that we eventually believe total suppression
of our emotions keeps us from losing our control. We survived our
childhood traumas by protecting ourselves from pain and unhealthy
people. This worked well in those destructive relationships. But what
happens when you are around healthy people? Do you use the same
survival skills?

Most of us think survival skill behaviors are the same as relationship skill behaviors. They are not. Bringing survival skills into a relationship means you only expect to survive the experience, not to grow or enhance your life. In your relationships with women, is one of you trying to maintain a healthy balance while the other is merely trying to survive?

> *My most growth-producing relationship has been with a son of an alcoholic. However, the intensity and turmoil can be too much. It is overwhelming even for me, the daughter of alcoholics. He possesses uncanny sensitivity, too much at times. I believe if the boundary issues and self-esteem could be healed, it would be a beautiful, heavenly relationship.*
>
> DIANE

What do you "hear" when you read these comments? Do you listen, or do you rationalize as you read? Does it seem that the comments were made out of concern, or do they strike you as "nagging"? How you interpret them has a lot to do with whether or not you are willing to listen.

We need to listen to ourselves in order to hear others. Most of the things we hear from others we have already told ourselves. Will we use the feedback from this chapter, or simply ignore the women's comments? When we choose to do nothing, we are not only ignoring the people who love us and try to communicate with us, but continuing to ignore ourselves and our unmet needs.

Following are the results of a survey taken by Sam Keen in which women were asked to identify the characteristics of "ideal" men and "inferior" men.[1] As you read this list, what do you hear inside you? Are you listening?

Traits of Ideal Men	Percent of Respondents
Caring/loving	65
Intelligent	34
Moral/honest	29
Sensitive	29
Family man	20

Traits of Inferior Men	
Egocentric	34
Immoral	30
Violent	19
Greedy	15
Insensitive	15
Stupid	15

AFTERTHOUGHTS

> *Men always want to be a woman's first love; women have a more subtle instinct: what they like is to be a man's last romance.*
>
> ANONYMOUS

> *If you judge people, you have no time to love them.*
>
> MOTHER TERESA

> *Love doesn't sit there like a stone, it has to be made, like bread; remade all the time, made new.*
>
> URSULA K. LEGUIN

> *When one door of happiness closes, another opens; but often we look so long at the closed door that we do not see the one which has been opened for us.*
>
> HELEN KELLER

> *We're all in this together—by ourselves.*
>
> LILY TOMLIN

CHAPTER TEN

Parenting: Our Fathers Never Had to Do These Things

It's hard for me to look my son in the eye and tell him that I love him. My father often told me that he loved me, but he was never there to back that claim up.

JULIO

Before you became a father, did you promise yourself that you would be a better father than yours was? Did you think that if you ever had children you would be involved in their lives, would spend time with them and listen to them with patience and praise? When you held your child for the first time, watched your boy take his first steps, or heard your daughter say "Daddy," did you find yourself renewing that promise?

As silent sons, we are long on desire but short on guidance. We are, however, strong in our conviction. We are determined to stop the dysfunctional pattern that started generations ago. We believe that our families *are* going to be different, and it seems that we, both as silent sons and simply as men, represent a transitional generation of fathers. Whether we like it or not, the role of fatherhood is definitely changing.

Years ago Margaret Mead, the famous anthropologist, stated that fatherhood was a social invention, implying that the family group had to find some reason to keep the father within the family.[1] This "invention" dictates that we be good providers, disciplinarians, and part-time readers of the daily newspaper. The societal concept of traditional fathering was very restricted and did not challenge a man to develop his innate potential as a nurturer, teacher, or caretaker of children.

John, a 41-year-old postal worker, remembers being a young father and taking his son for walks around the block every day. The Coles, an elderly couple, lived down the street from John and his family. Every time John walked past their house, old Mr. Cole would stop and talk with him. He always told John how lucky he was to be able to walk with his son, and often repeated a story about how when his daughter was young, he worked six and sometimes seven days a week as a maintenance man for the UpJohn Company. He said the job required him to be on call all the time. He always told John how much he looked forward to Saturday nights because, if all went well, he didn't have to work. He could stay home with his family. He talked about how Saturday night was his chance to feed the baby, give her a bath, read to her, and put her to bed. John never knew if Mr. Cole repeated that story a lot because he didn't remember telling him, or because he was trying to tell him to remember what was important. Either way, John heard Mr. Cole's message, but also heard his pain. The man had wanted to be there for his daughter and couldn't. He had wanted to be more than a paycheck. He had wanted to be a father.

In the past, most men fulfilled their roles as fathers by remaining on the periphery of their families, rarely getting involved in their children's lives. Everyone simply assumed that not only was this the way it should be, it was the way men wanted it. However, as you will see in this chapter, this certainly is not the case with silent sons who are fathers. We want to be involved, but we don't know how to make it happen. We also have an inferiority complex, because we constantly hear these things:[2]

- Fathers are uninterested in and uninvolved with children.
- Fathers prefer non-caretaking roles.

- Fathers are less nurturing toward infants than mothers.
- Fathers are less competent caregivers than mothers.

Research *does not* support these myths with regard to the current generation of fathers.[3] Studies have found that fathers do not differ significantly from mothers in their interest toward infants and children—that in fact they *like* being involved with their children and are as nurturing as mothers toward them. Though they may not engage in active caregiving as much as mothers, they are competent when they have to be.

Social changes have occurred over the past twenty-five years that have led to the change in fathers' roles. The womens' movement, the necessity for two-income families, social expectations for fathers to become more involved with their children, and, an awareness among men of the importance of being an effective parent are some of the reasons for these advances.

But this transition is not easy. We as fathers are being asked to shift from the way our fathers and grandfathers parented to this new, seemingly all-inclusive fatherhood. New fathers still maintain many of the responsibilities and expectations of the old father model, but in addition they are supposed to be emotionally and psychologically involved with their children and to share equally in the care and concern for their well-being.

We can expand our roles as fathers, but first we must expand ourselves as men. To do so, we must break away from the stereotypical images of manhood and fatherhood. Though not impossible, this does cause a tremendous amount of stress. The territory of emotional involvement is foreign to many men. And, as when we approach all new territory, we can either ask directions or hope to find our way by chance. As hard as this might be for the functional male, it will be even harder for many silent sons.

As this book has documented, silent sons have special problems with emotional expression and overcoming a limited perception of what it is to be male. Silent sons who want to make the transition also have to deal with the burden of poor parental role models and with the unresolved issues of their own childhood. Children need healthy parents. It would be ideal for all of us to become healthier before we become fathers, but most of us don't, and our kids suffer the consequences of our on-the-job training. Don't wait to change. Do it now. While you're waiting, your children are growing.

When you become emotionally involved positively with your children, you open a whole new door in your life, and this door swings both ways. You will open up a whole new world for your children—namely, knowing their father. In return you will find a whole new world of amazement, love, and self-worth in your children. And you will find a whole new wellspring of undiscovered potential within you. Children will teach you many things. They will teach you that you are capable of using your talents. They will teach you to feel emotions you didn't know you had, to smile inside, and to recognize the many ways there are to love. They will make you feel good about yourself in ways you thought you had lost. Most importantly, they will show you that you cannot run out of love.

Admittedly, every day with your children is not the most blessed event on earth. There are times when you are exhausted or frustrated, but this doesn't mean that you are tired of your children. The unconditional love of your child and memories of the good times carry you through while you cope with the problems of fatherhood, both new and old.

As transitional fathers, we are being asked to break the chain of past generations and to muffle the voices of our own fathers still echoing in our heads. Silent son transitional fathers are also asked to break the chain of their dysfunctional childhoods. If we cannot reprogram our emotional tapes, the chain of silence will continue—not only for us but for our children. If we don't change, we won't hear the music of our children. All children want someone to listen to their songs. If you don't, they will only sing so long and then they will stop. And then they will be silent, just like their fathers.

SILENT SONS AS FATHERS

As a silent son, are you worried that you are too handicapped to make a good father? Did you ever think you might have an advantage? Your dysfunctional parents may have taught you some good things, such as how to take care of yourself, how to respect other people, and how to be independent. They also probably taught you how a parent should *not* act. If you are aware that you would like to be a better parent, then you know what you want. Although you may not express yourself openly right now, you harbor a great deal of empathy and sensitivity within you. That means you have two very important qualities needed to be a good father. What you need to do now is to put them into practice.

You are not alone in your struggle to accomplish this. Most of the silent sons I interviewed had a high level of awareness of parenting issues and problems, but needed a push to change, because fears and concerns of failing held them back.

How much silent sons can learn will depend on the degree to which you can work through both your past and your fears, which will determine how well you do. It will also determine how well your children will do.

Let's examine some of the most common concerns of silent son fathers. Many of these concerns are shared by all fathers, but were felt more deeply by those silent sons I interviewed. The problems they identified were: (1) fear of repeating the mistakes of their parents, (2) lack of parenting skills, (3) not knowing how to enforce discipline and set appropriate limits, (4) lack of confidence in their ability to meet their children's needs, and (5) fear of giving too much to their children.

REPEATING MISTAKES

> *My role model was an alcoholic dysfunctional father. He taught me that a father uses degradation, sarcasm, put-downs, and threats to ensure what he considered appropriate behavior from me. Tired of being the family scapegoat, I eventually told him where he could stick his attitude, but then he responded with physical abuse. As a parent in recovery I have had to work very hard to replace his negative example and develop new skills of my own.*
>
> LARRY

175

Do you ever hear yourself sounding like your father? And does it scare the hell out of you? Do you think you are behaving differently than he ever did, but in times of stress find yourself practically replicating the things your father did? Do you fear you can't be different? If so, you are not alone. The greatest parenting fear for silent sons I spoke with was repeating the mistakes of their childhood with their own children.

Silent sons also fear confronting their feelings about their childhood, which their own children inadvertently force to the surface of memory. For silent sons, parenting is a constant reminder of childhood. Old tapes get played and old behaviors find their way out of the closet. If you are a silent son father who wants change for his children, you will need to work through your own childhood issues and learn alternative parenting skills. It is difficult to do things differently for your child while you're working from the same old patterns. What is the first step toward change? List the things you learned that you do not want your children to learn. Your list might include such negative lessons as: Keep your feelings to yourself; be afraid of your father; parents are too busy to listen; business always comes before family; what the neighbors say is more important than how you feel; it's too embarrassing to have friends come over to the house. Once you make your list, think about which of your behaviors might teach such unwanted lessons. Do you remember how you learned them?

Very few parents purposely try to harm their children. Parenting mistakes are instilled very subtly, usually through the repetition of communication patterns. Are you impatient or intolerant of childish behaviors? Are you more likely to talk with your kids only when you have something negative to say? Do you often criticize, but seldom offer praise?

> *At times I hear my father's stern voice in my own. I consciously work at controlling that. I don't want to re-create the addiction cycle in my children. Probably the most negative time for them is when my wife and I fight and I explode over seemingly trivial situations.*
>
> GUS

As fathers, we are the link between our past and our children. We all want to leave an inheritance for our children which will help them and make their lives easier. If you want your children to inherit emotional strength and positive family patterns, you need to break the cycle. It won't work to merely use the old saying, "Do as I say, not as I do." That's probably what you heard yourself. In order to raise healthy kids you need to be able to model healthy behaviors. To do that, you must learn them first yourself. Learn to take care of yourself; you will in turn take care of your kids.

PARENTING SKILLS

Raising sons—how do I do it? What's a real father like?
GEORGE

Like many silent son fathers, you might find yourself frequently feeling that you don't know what you're doing. When this occurs, you can either let someone else shoulder the bulk of your responsibilities, repeat only what you know, or go out and learn parenting skills. When you aren't aware of alternative parenting techniques, you are condemned to repeat the past.

I started my journey as a single-parent father by *knowing* I knew very little. I spent time with other parents, asked many questions, read a lot, went to support meetings, and shared my fears and concerns with other single parents. I did not stop doing everything in my life because I became a father. Rather, I did them with Jason whenever I could. I remember I played on a softball team at the time. I told the guys I still wanted to play, but it would be hard to come to all of the practices. They said they understood, I could still play the games, and besides, they said, none of them wanted to be in my shoes. So much for total male support! They could handle letting me play softball, but single parenting? They weren't so sure. However, they did help, and maybe Jason brought out the best in them at times. When I showed up for the games I was in uniform, but had a few additional items other than my glove; I also carried a diaper bag, bottles, toys, and one small son. When I was in the field, one of the guys on the bench watched Jason. I know this is the last thing the guys thought they

177

would ever do that season, but they did help. Maybe they all learned a little about coming together, something about babies, and a lot about themselves.

The point is, you can learn. You can be a good father if you are a good learner. You can learn to nurture with the best of them. Many of us are not sure if we can nurture and still feel like men. Why not? Nurturing does not mean doing it the same as women. Men have their own ways of nurturing. The important thing is not how you nurture, but that your kids feel nurtured.

If you allow yourself to become a healthy father, the best of you will emerge. One of the most important things to learn, however, is that the best thing a father can do for his children is to get along with their mother. It is difficult to be a good father if you are not a good husband. When the spouse relationship is solid, the parenting stands a better chance. In fact, it was found that good fathering is closely tied to the success of the marriage relationship.[4] If you are a single father, the best thing to do is to take care of yourself physically and emotionally. This includes maintaining healthy relationships.

DISCIPLINE AND SETTING LIMITS

Silent son fathers have difficulty enforcing discipline and setting limits for children. Not having had enough experience with good role models, being exposed to very rigid standards, and not knowing what is normal or average can lead to problems. For silent sons I have talked to, the greatest of these problems appeared to be inconsistency— going too far sometimes and not far enough other times. Inconsistency only confuses your children. Children need to know what to expect in order to understand rules and develop security. Can you remember the chaos and inconsistency in your family while you were growing up? Can you remember getting too little attention one day and too much another?

You can't vacillate between wanting to be your children's father and their friend. You are their father. They can make their own friends. The problem with discipline and setting limits is worse when you don't feel good about yourself or secure in your role as father. If you suffer from low self-esteem, it is easy to feel guilty when you set limits for your children. When they get mad at you it makes you feel rejected. You fear you will lose their love, but if you don't set limits you will lose your children. Research on children indicates that setting limits is better for children than absolute freedom. Your children look to you for guidance whether you realize it or not. Think back: How many times in your own childhood did you wish you had parental support, especially from your father?

Setting limits and discipline doesn't have to be negative. Setting limits helps establish boundaries, teach right and wrong, and instill a set of values. If you don't know what normal guidelines are, ask other parents. Join a fathers' group or a parents' group. If you are having trouble setting limits for your children, particularly if they are teenagers, go to a family counselor to work out fair limits and healthy discipline patterns. It might take a lot for you to go, but it will take a lot more out of you to raise a teenager who is out of control.

Setting limits teaches your children a sense of justice by helping them learn that actions have consequences. One of the most important things I learned from my father was how to be fair. Yes, he was rigid, he set limits, and he would say, "You do this, period!"—but he enforced rules fairly.

Once when I was in seventh grade I went on a Saturday afternoon hike with the guys. There is nothing like setting a bunch of 12-year-olds free in the woods. We hiked to the top of a mountain in Pennsylvania and built a fire to cook lunch. My job was to find water, but when I returned everyone was quiet and acting a little weird. Suddenly I looked around for my new jacket (which I had left when I went to get the water) and it was gone. I said, "All right, where's my coat?" In response I got a chorus of "I don't know"s and some stifled laughs. My "friends" had decided to play catch with my coat over the fire. Sure enough, it fell in. Eventually I was handed the remains; a burnt zipper and a few fragments of material. Only I knew that what I really had was major grief waiting for me at home.

Sure enough, when I got home the first thing my mother asked was, "Where's your jacket?" I reached into my pocket and pulled out the fragments and the zipper of what once a new spring coat. After my mother hit the roof, she finished her familiar dissertation with the dreaded immortal words: "Wait till your father gets home." Wonderful, I thought, now we're going to play beat the clock until we beat the boy. When my father came home, my mother told him everything. I figured, This is it, it's over, but then I heard my father say in a very controlled voice, "Well, sometimes boys will be boys." My father walked to my room, looked in, and said, "Don't let it happen again." I realized then and there I would live another day and that there truly was a God. I also realized that as strict as my father was, he was fair.

As fathers today, we need to teach our children that there are rules to abide by and consequences of their actions, but we also need to teach them fairness. In order to do this, we must be fair to ourselves by acknowledging our own limitations and trying to overcome them. We can't teach limits if we don't have any ourselves. We can't teach fairness if we are not fair to our children. The rules, values, and attitudes we teach our children must serve them well even when we are not around. These lessons are not limited to what our children do in front of us. The power of the lessons is in how they behave when we are not watching. They need to learn to say yes and no, so as fathers we must teach them well. Our lessons are only as good as the teacher.

MEETING YOUR CHILDREN'S NEEDS

Do you ever feel that you can't reach your children? Do you ever wonder if you understand them? Do you often feel that you are not equipped to be a father? Are you afraid that you cannot give what your children need from you? You may feel that you can provide their physical needs and discipline, but may be uncertain when it comes to their emotional and nurturing needs. In order to meet these needs, you must be able not only to give *beyond* yourself, but also to give *of* yourself. That is, you need to be able to give emotionally if you are to meet emotional needs.

> *Perhaps it would have been easier if I had a daughter. I hugged and kissed both my sons frequently as children, but I never remember saying I loved them. I always believed if I showed them love, I would never have to say it.*
>
> DARYL

Children need their parents to be able to identify with their feelings, but this is difficult if as a parent you cannot identify with your own. When a child needs emotional support, he or she doesn't want cold, mechanical advice. The child wants an emotional response that communicates an understanding. If your son strikes out in a critical little league game, that is not the time for a lesson in batting, but in handling emotions. You may help him become a better hitter, but you can really help him learn to be a better person.

Some of the silent son fathers I interviewed felt it was difficult for them to meet their children's needs because they had difficulty expressing affection. All children need love and affection from their fathers, and being silent sons does not excuse us from giving these things. Remember, our pasts should not be their problem. Withholding affection from children is dangerous. Before long, they are establishing their own intimate, and healthy or unhealthy interaction patterns. The sooner we show affection, the better for us and our children. If we wait too long, it might take a major breakthrough to reverse a pattern.

Sometimes we fear that boys are too old or daughters are too mature, but a healthy hug is always welcome at the right time. If you wait too long to put your arm around your child, it won't feel right for either of you when you finally do. You will both sense the loss of a past opportunity.

> *The most difficult thing for me has been knowing how to balance the nurturing part of me with other male characteristics.*
>
> SAM

Men can and do meet the emotional needs of children, sometimes very well. It is important not to think that we are less masculine if we try to be nurturing or sensitive. Many silent sons admitted they held back from being tender or affectionate because they weren't sure it was masculine. The true potential of a man is actually expanded when he reaches out beyond himself.

How do you feel when your children express their emotions? Let your children know it is important for them to express their feelings freely. You may be uncomfortable with your children's emotions if you are uncomfortable with your own. Children can sense this and will start to shut down. Emotional needs can't be met if they are not expressed one way or another—let them open up. Our pain can impede our children's emotions since if we hold back, they tend to hold back. If you are overwhelmed by your own pain, get help, and do it now. Seek out professional advice. If you hold back your feelings, don't be surprised if one day you ask them, "Why don't you talk to me? Tell me what you're feeling," and they don't respond. You will then feel the strength of the wall that keeps you out, just as they felt yours.

> *I have no basis for comparison as to what is right, only*
> *what I remember as being wrong.*
>
> JAMES

There are many types of child abuse, though people tend to focus on the physical. One type of abuse is failure to meet a child's emotional needs. This is called emotional neglect. Many parents engage in emotional neglect and verbal abuse and aren't even aware of it. If you kept track of your conversations with your children, would you discover that the negative comments outweigh the positive ones? Are you more likely to speak to them only to criticize or correct? Perhaps you sometimes say too much and at other times not enough. The next time your son looks at you and you know he needs you to say something, or you feel the need to reach him, take the risk and tell him what you feel. You are both worth it.

> *I keep feeling like I'm cheating my daughter out of*
> *"quality time," since I've been doing the "Uncle Daddy"*
> *role for most of her life. I may not be able to meet her*
> *needs if she ever developed a serious problem such as*
> *chemical dependency.*
>
> CHET

Children teach us that the essence of a relationship is doing things together, and for them this usually means playing together. True, children can play by themselves, but there's nothing like having someone to play with, especially if it's dad. But many silent sons felt they didn't know how to play. The ability to play requires growth. It requires you to be creative, to let yourself go, to use your imagination, and to relax. It requires a commitment to spend time with your child. Are you uncomfortable taking time out to play with your children? Is it because you don't know how to play, or because playing takes time away from other "important" things? Children don't ask for much when they ask you to play, but they do demand your time. All children know that the one thing they want most from their fathers is the one thing fathers think they have the least of—time. If you don't have time for your children, who does? Do you think someone else's time spent with your child is as meaningful? No way! Don't fool yourself by rationalizing that you don't spend much time with your kids, but that the time you do spend is quality time. What is "quality time," anyway? The phrase certainly wasn't invented by kids. Can you remember what was quality time with your parents and what wasn't? Neither can your kids. What do kids call the time you spend with them? Simply time.

Perhaps you decide to set aside certain times for your children. That's great—it's extra time together. But don't forget the ordinary time when you are together. A lot happens there too.

Spending time together is a prerequisite for bonding. Bonding with your children does not occur physiologically in fathers to the degree it does for mothers. You didn't carry them inside of you for nine months, but you do carry them in your arms and in your heart. Bonding with your children means you make an emotional connection with them and about them. You and I know you can live in the same house with your father but never connect. But some of us may also know you can live miles away from your father today and feel closer to him than ever. Your children do not want to live with you as though you are miles apart. They will leave you soon enough. And when they do leave, they will only be able to take your emotional gifts with them. These gifts will ensure that your relationship continues to grow. These gifts will continue to meet their needs. Don't let silence claim another child. You are in control of your children's legacy. Take charge and meet their needs before it's too late.

GIVING TOO MUCH

*I'm always afraid I'm making a mistake with my son,
and that I'll really screw him up. I am afraid if I tell him
too often or too excessively how very much I love him I
will harm him.*

PHIL

Are you afraid of giving your children too much? Do you want to give them everything you didn't get? You give too much when you give your children everything you can and don't allow them to learn for themselves.

I can remember sitting at lunch with two friends who were also silent sons and fathers. The three of us were talking about our children, how much we did with them, how different we were from our own fathers, how much kids had today, and still we were wondering if we were doing enough. It was ironic that each of us did more than our fathers ever did, but still we had our doubts. All fathers have doubts, but when we are doing our best we must accept it is the best we can do. When we give too much to our children, we are sabotaging what we are trying to teach them. As fathers we want our children to be able to assume responsibility and to become well-balanced adults. Ask yourself if you often find yourself doing any of the following:

- I let my children get by with rude or impolite behavior because they are upset or it's an inconvenient time for me to correct them.
- I allow my children to avoid or withdraw from activities because they complain they are "too hard" or "not fun."
- I constantly give my children money or buy things that they want.
- When my children neglect their chores or responsibilities, I usually do them myself but I complain about it loudly.
- My children often talk me out of disciplinary measures.
- If my child damages or loses property through personal negligence, I automatically replace it if my child gets upset.
- If my child gets into trouble, I often intercede on his or her behalf.

- I sometimes cross the line between supporting my child and doing a job for her or him.
- I am willing to stretch ethical boundaries to keep my child happy.

According to Bruce Baldwin, a psychologist, these are classic ways of giving your children too much and sabatoging what you want to teach. He suggests teaching our children the following three key beliefs:[5]

- I am accountable for my behavior and the consequences of my behavior at all times.
- There is a direct relationship between my efforts and the rewards of my efforts.
- I know how to make good things happen for me in positive and ethical ways.

One indicator of giving too much is when you find yourself acting outside the role as father. This occurs when you are trying to be both mother and father, or to be both friend and father. Over the years, research has shown that children are best adjusted when each parent fulfills his and her respective roles well. A healthy father and a healthy mother complement each other in their parenting. Behaviors in parents that complement one another let children know that their parents work as a team. In a two-parent family, if one parent does all the work children don't get a healthy sense of shared parenting responsibilities. Although gender role changes are occurring, children still look to their mothers for certain nurturing behaviors and to their fathers for certain instructional behaviors. This expands the role models for children and gives them better alternatives for healthy behaviors. If either parent crosses his or her parental boundaries, it is likely to be uncomfortable for both parents and does not benefit the children.

Giving too much is usually an attempt to overcompensate for past behaviors. Your motivation shouldn't be behind you but in front of you. Healthy fathers fulfill their roles because they want to. If you are pushed into your role, your parenting motivations can be based on anger, revenge, frustration, and pain. When this occurs, you are attempting to meet your needs, not your child's.

Unfortunately, we live in an age when giving too much comes too easily. This is especially true of material things. For example, kids love to get toys, and there are more toys now than you and I ever thought possible. But we also know that giving too much does not teach responsibility. It can teach children to expect too much and to become resentful when these expectations are not met. We must avoid giving too much as a way of compensating for not communicating with our kids or not spending enough time with them. Maybe the gifts our children really want can't be purchased. What they really want is you.

Think of what it is you really want to give your children. You want to give them things that will last, don't you? Toys, no matter how great, remain toys and eventually break. As a father you can give your children a gift of great and lasting value—guidelines and attitudes that will help them in their lives. Sure, it would be nice to leave them a house, car, and money, but without your mentoring, what will they have when these things break down, get old, or run out? The best gifts you can give your children will remain long after you are gone. Have you ever thought about what messages you would like to leave with your sons or daughters? If you could leave them a legacy of lessons, what would they be? I challenge you to list ten lessons you want to teach your children. Try it by completing this sentence: I would like my children to:

1. _____
2. _____
3. _____
4. _____
5. _____
6. _____
7. _____
8. _____
9. _____
10. _____

What did you learn from this? That you have goals for your children? Perhaps, but more importantly, that you have goals as a father?

Your goal is to teach, not merely to give. Giving is an expression of yourself, which is good, but it is an adjunct to being a father, not a substitute for it. A gift is not a gift unless it can be received. Our children need to learn how to be healthy receivers. That is the best gift we can give them.

Just to show you that I practice what I preach, here is my list to my children:

1. Be fair to yourself and others.
2. Respect people.
3. Listen to your coach—others can see things you can't.
4. Learn to play.
5. Find a job, but find what you like to do first.
6. Believe in God, and believe in yourself.
7. Love your family, respect your spouse, enjoy your children.
8. Do what's right, not what's popular.
9. Open presents on Christmas morning; it's more fun.
10. I love you.

AFTERTHOUGHTS

> The most important thing a father can do for his children is to love their mother.
>
> THEODORE HESBURGH

> If a man is fortunate he will, before he dies, gather up as much as he can of his civilized heritage and transmit it to his children.
>
> WILL DURANT

> To bring up a child in the way he should go, travel that way yourself once in a while.
>
> JOSH BILLINGS

Your children need your presence more than your presents.

JESSE JACKSON

Don't be a pal to your son. Be his father. What child needs a 40-year-old for a friend?

AL CAPP

CHAPTER ELEVEN

Our Jobs: Occupation, Addiction, or Mistress?

Without work all life goes rotten. But when work is soulless, the life stifles and dies.
ALBERT CAMUS

Remember when you were a boy and people used to ask, "What do you want to be when you grow up?" Can you imagine what they would have thought or how they would have reacted if you had just said, "Content, healthy, and human"?

We have been socialized to become "workers." We were taught that having a good job means having a good life. Our jobs are a big part of our lives, and there is no denying it. The question is, how much does your job dominate your identity? Has it *become* your identity? In their conversations with me, silent sons talked about their jobs a lot.

Some silent sons saw their jobs as an occupation, something they were good at, something that they had to do, and something they enjoyed. While they saw their jobs as a part of who they were, they also believed there was a lot more to them than what they did. These men had a healthy view of their jobs because they had a healthy view of themselves.

Other silent sons were workaholics—addicted to their jobs. Their entire identity was a result of the rush of the job, not of their self-esteem. These men felt good about themselves only when they were working, and they had few other interests outside of work. Workaholic silent sons also heavily identified with a narrow male image. They equated their worth with a paycheck.

The third group of silent sons saw their jobs as a source of power, intrigue, and excitement, feelings that they believed they could not find elsewhere. These men had a strong desire to keep their occupation totally separate from their family, and it was not uncommon for their partners to complain that they thought more about their job than they did their family. These men were seduced by their jobs and led astray from their other responsibilities. They related to work as to a mistress, willing to do anything to please it and revealing a part of themselves in the job that no one else ever saw. It seemed their job brought out their passion and only then did they feel "alive." They thought their job "understood" them. It met their needs. Though their partner might have realized they were not having an affair, it certainly felt as if they were.

Most of us derive a great deal of satisfaction and self-esteem from our work. I myself like to accomplish things and I am proud of my accomplishments. Like many other silent sons, however, I went through a time where my work was my *only* source of self-worth. I strongly identified with the motto "You are what you do and you are nothing if you don't." I worked hard and I worked all the time, so I didn't feel like a "nothing." Even when I was off, I was on.

I learned several things from this time in my life. I realized I was capable of working all the time. I found I could do a lot of things and that people paid attention to my accomplishments. But I also realized it wasn't enough.

When we realize that our accomplishments aren't enough, we are faced with two choices. We can work even harder to see if that will help fill the void, or we can look for other things to add meaning to our lives. It is difficult for men to find worth outside of their work. In order to do this, we must expand our perceptions about ourselves and about the things that lend meaning to our lives.

When you don't get enough out of your job, where do you look—at yourself or at your job? If you look solely to your job to provide the meaning in your life, your job becomes all things to you and you must be all things to your job. If you feel this way, you are a prime candidate to become a workaholic.

A workaholic is addicted to his job and feels good about himself only when he is working. To him, work equals worth and anything besides working is seen as an unworthy activity. Unfortunately, he judges everything, including himself, this way. The workaholic does not think that anything or anyone is as important as his job. His message is heard by everyone around him. He knows the high price of success, but he is not the only one who pays it. Just as other addicts affect those around them, so do workaholics. They're usually just too busy to notice.

What about you? Are you a workaholic? Do you put your job ahead of everything and everyone? Can you express yourself beyond your job? Ironically, a man can feel he has reached his full growth potential by being successful in his job, but this same man can also feel empty when he is not working. He has really reached only one of his potentials, and deep inside he knows it is not enough.

Answer the following questions to assess your workaholic potential. Be honest, and don't skip this section because it takes too long to complete. What else should you be doing—working?

1. T F I frequently meet people who are in authority but who really are no better than I.
2. T F Once I start a job I have no peace until I finish.
3. T F I like to tell people exactly what I think.
4. T F Whereas most people are overly conscious of their feelings, I like to deal with facts.
5. T F I worry about business and financial matters.
6. T F I often have anxiety about something or someone.
7. T F I sometimes become so preoccupied by a thought that I cannot get it out of my mind.
8. T F I find it difficult to go to bed or sleep because of things that bother me.
9. T F I have periods during which I cannot sit or lie down—I need to be doing something.

10. T F My mind is often occupied by thoughts about what I have done wrong or not completed.
11. T F My concentration is not what it used to be.
12. T F My personal appearance is always neat and clean.
13. T F I feel irritated when I see another person's messy desk or cluttered room.
14. T F I am more comfortable in a neat, clean, and orderly room than in a messy one.
15. T F I cannot get through a day or a week without a schedule or a list of jobs to do.
16. T F I believe that the man who works the hardest and longest deserves to get ahead.
17. T F If my job demands more time, I will cut out pleasurable activities to see that it gets done.
18. T F My conscience often bothers me about things I have done in the past.
19. T F There are things which I have done which would embarrass me greatly if they became public knowledge.
20. T F When I was a student I felt uncomfortable unless I got the highest grade.
21. T F It is my view that many people become confused because they don't bother to find out all the facts.
22. T F I frequently feel angry without knowing what or who is bothering me.
23. T F I can't stand to have my checkbook or financial matters out of balance.
24. T F I think talking about feelings to others is a waste of time.
25. T F There have been times when I became preoccupied with washing my hands or keeping things clean.
26. T F I like always to be in control of myself and to know as much as possible about things happening around me.
27. T F I have few or no close friends with whom I share warm feelings openly.
28. T F I feel that the more you know about future events, the better off you are.

29. T   F   There are things I have done which I will never live down.

30. T   F   I always avoid being late to a meeting or an appointment.

31. T   F   I rarely give up until the job has been completely finished.

32. T   F   I often expect things of myself that no one else would ask of himself.

33. T   F   I sometimes worry about whether I was wrong or made a mistake.

34. T   F   I would like others to see me as not having any faults.

35. T   F   The groups and organizations I join have strict rules and regulations.

36. T   F   I believe there are commandments and rules to live by and we fail if we don't follow all of them.

Count your number of true statements. If you scored 10 or less, you are a fairly relaxed man. If you scored between 11 and 20, you are average. If you scored 21 or more you, have strong tendencies toward becoming a workaholic.[1]

CONCERNS OF SILENT SONS ON THE JOB

Silent sons I talked with were aware that many of their personality traits and issues go to work with them every day. Silent sons possess many positive qualities which make them very successful, but often these same qualities can lead to early burnout. For example, not wanting to finish a project until it is absolutely perfect might get you promoted, but you might also be too exhausted for the next project. Your willingness to help everyone is admirable, but your inability to say no has caused you to become overextended and spread too thinly. Your intense drive for success has made it difficult for others to be around you.

These are only a few of the many paradoxes plaguing silent sons. In the following sections we will discuss some of the chief concerns they voiced. Their problems on the job included: feeling they were not good enough, lacking interpersonal work skills, not being team players, and alcoholism.

NOT GOOD ENOUGH

> *I often "cover my ass" more than I need to. I find criticism hard to take. I also feel I must be perfect and do no wrong, which adds much additional pressure to my work day.*
>
> RALPH

Do you often do your best at work and feel it just isn't good enough? Is it good enough for your boss but not for you? Some silent sons admitted to being perfectionists at work. They held themselves accountable to exceptionally high standards—not the ones in the office, but the ones in their heads. Does this sound like you? Do you think there is one set of standards for everyone else and one for you? What do you do with these standards? Do you drive yourself to higher levels of perfection, which are seldom achieved, and often feel like a failure? Or worse yet, do you project your standards on others?

Several silent sons told me they often feel like imposters at work because they are not there for the same reasons as everyone else. They know they are marching to their own drum and it keeps beating Do more, Do more, Do better, Do better. The thing they fail to realize is that the only thing getting beat is them. Perfectionists can never be happy since few things—and even fewer men—are ever perfect. Aiming at perfection means you are always trying to prove yourself— but do you know who you are trying to prove yourself to? Is it someone at work, someone from your past, yourself, or maybe your father? Whoever it is, the motivation comes from more than just your job. Maybe the job is just a place to play this motivation out. Have you ever felt that if you accomplish just one more thing, someone important will notice? Do you believe that if what you do is acceptable, then you are acceptable? It is never enough, though, is it? Looking to your job for the answers means you are asking the wrong questions. Job satisfaction is not in the job, it's in the person.

Not feeling that you are good enough is also related to fear of criticism. Are you overly sensitive to criticism? If someone says something negative about an aspect of your work, do you immediately discount all that you have done? Do you think that for something to be acceptable it must be 100 percent perfect, and it only takes 1 percent for it to be wrong? When we are overly sensitive to criticism, we take it more personally than professionally. No one likes to have his work criticized, but unfortunately it always occurs. You can win an Academy Award and there will always be people who don't like the movie. If you fear excessive criticism on the job, it is probably because you fear that whoever is criticizing you is *right*. It means your confidence is easily destroyed. It means you have low self-worth.

Being good enough obviously means you are doing well in your job, but it also means you are feeling good about yourself. Too many silent sons leave work every day wondering about their worth. These same men usually do well, but seldom believe it. They know that something is missing, be it self-approval, an internal sense of worth, the conviction to accept that they have done their best, or a feeling that there is much more to them than what they do from eight to five. A job means a lot to a man, but when there is something missing on the inside you will seldom find it in your job. A job should add to our expression and creativity as men, not be used in lieu of it.

Interpersonal Skills

> *Many times a man is rewarded in the working world for being aggressive, achieving great things, and putting on a front of competency, but these may be compensatory behaviors or even destructive behaviors. Being vulnerable, insightful, or self-critical is not acceptable.*
>
> Leon

How well do you relate to people on the job? One of the biggest problems for silent sons is learning to deal directly with people at work. I often heard silent sons say that when they didn't deal directly with coworkers they felt as if they were re-creating their dysfunctional families in the office. This parallel manifested itself in emotional manipulation, inability to express feelings, inability to delegate authority, rigidity, and even in bringing personal problems to work. These are the same patterns dysfunctional families exhibit.

Most men and most silent sons believe you cannot show your feelings on the job. Their motto? Don't let them see you sweat, don't blink, don't wince, be strong.

Wendell, age 34, is a fireman. He likes his job and enjoys being with the other firemen. He says that most of the conversations in the firehouse are superficial. Everyone keeps up their guard. The only time anyone ever talks about emotions or fears is when a fellow fireman gets hurt, and then they do so very guardedly. Wendell states, "I'm a fireman and macho is the major block to learning to be anything else. We're all rescuers and we can rescue ourselves. We're tough and strong. We don't need help, we only give it."

Are you comfortable delegating authority, or do you believe it is easier to just do it yourself? Are you uncomfortable asking someone to help you? Do you think you communicate well with others at work, but seldom ask for what you need? As an officer in the military I can remember how uncomfortable I was asking someone to do something or giving orders. I usually just did it myself. Eventually it dawned on me that I was given a staff for a reason. Although many silent sons are very successful, many are not comfortable communicating with other people or having our own needs met. Obviously, we bring many of our interpersonal skills, or lack thereof, to work.

How rigid are you on the job? Are you a black-and-white thinker? Are you a risk taker, or do you try to avoid change and keep the boat safe? Do you stay in the harbor or go sailing? What kind of person are you to work for? Rigidity was exhibited by silent sons in several ways, such as how they treated women coworkers, how poorly they related to authority figures, and how strongly they needed to control everything. Many silent sons had difficulty with authority figures, as it is difficult to become autonomous early in life and then listen to someone else. Some saw authority figures as parent figures, still others saw them as people with the power to harm them. Many silent sons approached authority figures with caution and distrust.

Another set of interpersonal problems for silent sons arose from acting out their personal problems at work. This is not uncommon for many people. Stress off the job often means additional stress on the job. When this happens, we feel burned out even before we begin work. We start the day exhausted and irritable and are not sure why. Obviously, we are not concentrating as we should be, and we may also find it difficult to defend our ideas. For example, if you suffer from low self-esteem due to living in dysfunction, you are often unsure of yourself. It is easy for someone to attack or challenge your ideas when you don't feel good about yourself or you just don't have the motivation to stand up for yourself.

Occupationally, many of the most successful men come from dysfunctional families. These are silent sons who come alive at work because they are in a different environment and are exceptionally competent at separating themselves from their dysfunctional past. These men are not afraid of problems. They are not easily intimidated when things go wrong—they have had lots of crisis training. These are "take charge" men who use their "survival training" constructively.

If these men have problems in their lives, it is usually with their families. As silent sons they feel guilty for neglecting their families, but also admit they don't feel as comfortable there as they do at work. They feel adequate at work and inadequate at home, and solve this problem by spending more and more time away from home.

Their solution ultimately becomes the problem. They need to learn to use successful interpersonal skills from work at home. This is not an easy transition, but it's also not easy for their families, because even when silent sons are at home their work is there with them. Do the following behavior patterns describe you?

- Is your schedule always full of work-related activities, while family activities take second place?
- Are your accomplishments or work activities the dominant theme of your conversations? Can you talk about something else besides work?
- Is the word "no" missing in your vocabulary when it comes to a work request, but frequently used at home?
- Do you have difficulty resting or relaxing?

Team Player

We are taught from the time we are boys to be team players. We do it for the good of the team. We are told that too much individualism on the team leads to the title "hotdog." Good team players feel like a part of the team and on equal level with all the other players.

Many silent sons find it difficult to be a team player at work. Because they became autonomous at very early ages in order to survive, their survival instincts are stronger than their socialization as team players. Three of the most common barriers to being team players for silent sons I spoke with were a strong sense of independence, difficulty trusting others, and need for control over situations.

Independence and teamwork are conflicting terms. As a boy you are taught early: Be independent, take care of yourself, don't let anyone push you around, be your own man. But you are also taught to be a team player. Unfortunately, if you grew up in a dysfunctional family you were taught that being part of a team, such as your family, was not always something good. Maybe you had to protect yourself from your own team, that is, from your family. As a result, you became cautious and mistrustful of others because you always felt you had to look out for yourself. This learned independence now means that you prefer to do things on your own. To become a team player you have to learn all over again.

You may do all right in a team situation, but only if you're the captain. Many silent sons admitted they did not mind being on the team if they could be in charge. After all, being in charge reduces or eliminates many of the fears about being on a team. When you are in charge you are in control. Would you rather be in charge of a project or follow someone else's direction? In which situation are you most comfortable?

Alcoholism

I nearly lost my job to alcoholism, and it certainly ruined many career opportunities. As a salesman, there

*are always so many people drinking around me. The
healthier I become, the more uncomfortable I feel at my
place of work.*

SEAN

Hard work and hard drinking go hand in hand for many men, and alcoholism is often rationalized as just another occupational hazard. It is easier for men to deny they have a drinking problem when they can rationalize that it is part of their job: "Everyone drinks and it is expected of you." True. Businessmen are expected to make deals over martini lunches; a bottle of alcohol is considered an appropriate male gift. As much as this puts many men at risk for alcoholism, many silent sons are at an even higher risk, especially if they are sons of alcoholics. "There's so much drinking going on, it's all around me, everyone expects me to drink," was a common statement I heard.

Silent sons talked about two types of alcoholism problems on the job: their own or someone else's. Being around an alcoholic is uncomfortable enough. It is even worse if the alcoholic is your boss or if he or she reminds you of your alcoholic parent. You may feel the need to protect yourself or find ways to handle the emotions and memories that might arise from your past. There are a variety of agencies that offer help, suggestions, and support groups for you if you are in one of these situations.

However, the alcoholism I am most concerned with is your own. Men can find every reason in the world to drink, and you can find every rationalization for drinking too much. Do you have a drinking problem and don't want to admit it? Are things slowly slipping away at work, but you don't want to face it? These are tough issues and they are tough to face. Answer the following questions about your own drinking:

- Have you ever decided to stop drinking for a week or so, but only succeeded for a couple of days?
- Do you wish people would mind their own business about your drinking?
- Have you ever switched from one kind of drink to another in the hope that this would keep you from getting drunk?

199

- During the past year, have you had to have a drink upon awakening?
- Do you envy people who can drink without getting into trouble?
- Have you had problems connected with drinking during the past year?
- Has your drinking caused trouble at home?
- Do you ever try to get "extra" drinks at a party because you did not get enough?
- Do you tell yourself that you can stop drinking any time you want to, even though you keep getting drunk when you don't mean to?
- Have you missed days of work or school because of drinking?
- Do you have blackouts?
- Have you ever felt that your life would be better if you did not drink?

If you answered yes to four or more of the above questions, you probably have trouble with alcohol.[2] You need to get help. Nothing will rob you of your personal or professional potential faster than alcoholism. Things never get better with alcoholism—they only get worse. Alcoholism is an equal-opportunity destroyer. It claims too many lives. Don't let it take you. Get help and get it now.

PRESTIGE AND PAYCHECKS

Do you find yourself measuring your worth by the size of your paycheck? Do you justify long hours, stomach problems, and family tension because you are making money? I'm not talking about making enough money to live on, but rather pursuing money just for the sake of money. Too often we have been led to believe that our worth is in our wallets. Ironically, the harder we work the more narrowly our worth becomes defined. We value ourselves less as we value money more. And our value to others begins to drop as well. If we give our all to only one thing, we seldom have anything left for anything else or anyone else—including ourselves. When the job becomes everything, we must become everything to the job. When the job becomes everything, we believe we are nothing without it.

Each of us needs to value ourselves and then believe we are priceless—that is, realize there are some things about us that are valuable beyond money. Do you know what these qualities are? There are things in this world that money cannot buy. Are you one of them? If so, you know you value many other things as well.

I believe all men want to be valued, and this is especially true for silent sons. Our true value, however, does not come from others, but from ourselves. When we realize this, we will realize we have tremendous capacities beyond our jobs. We will realize that our jobs are only a part of us, and that a man's potential is measured by more than the number of zeros on his pay stub. It is measured by our abilities to seize the moment, take control of our lives, find meaning inside ourselves, laugh, love, receive, give, and enjoy life. None of these things can be bought. They are all worth more than money.

There must be more than a paycheck to determine our worth. Our jobs take a lot out of us. Most of the things they demand and require we cannot replace with money. We cannot buy more time. We cannot buy more days with our children. We cannot buy back our health. We cannot buy back a collapsed relationship. Take time out from your job to renew yourself. You need to replenish your spirit and your body. You cannot do these things at work, and you cannot do them by bringing more work home. You need to be healthy to have a healthy attitude about your job. Health is maintained by taking care of yourself. When was the last time you took *one* hour off for you? When was the last time you walked in the woods, went to a ball game, saw a movie, sat in church and listened to the silence, spent time with your children with no agenda, spent the day in your "Saturday pants" when it wasn't Saturday, or started something you always meant to do? If you let it your job will take everything, including your identity. Of all the men I have met or read about, I never heard it said that at the end of his life he wished he had worked more.

AFTERTHOUGHTS

Choose a job you love, and you will never have to work a day in your life.
                                        CONFUCIUS

Lack of something to feel important about is almost the greatest tragedy a man may have.
                                        ARTHUR E. MORGAN

You always pass failure on the way to success.
                                        MICKEY ROONEY

When you win, nothing hurts.
                                        JOE NAMATH

I am only an average man, but, by George, I work harder at it than the average man.
                                        THEODORE ROOSEVELT

CHAPTER TWELVE

Pain, Power, Peace, and Potential

In the depth of winter, I finally learned that within me lay an invincible summer.

ALBERT CAMUS

Ludwig van Beethoven was a silent son. He was severely abused as a boy by his alcoholic father, and he had an alcoholic mother who was sent away to a cloister.[1] He suffered many of the emotional and physical injuries common among silent sons. Yet he functioned, survived, and thrived in spite of his past. Even now, his work survives him and adds great beauty to this world. Beethoven *expressed* himself through his music. He allowed his creativity to flow, even though he was constantly plagued by his past. He himself struggled with alcoholism and other problems, but he went on to become one of the world's greatest composers.

The worst thing that could have happened to a composer happened to Beethoven. He eventually went deaf as a result of the beatings he received from his father. He lived in silence, but this did not stop him from expressing himself. Instead of feeling bitter or angry, he reached inside himself and continued to write music. In spite of all that happened to him, he was still able to find beauty in this world and, more importantly, in himself. He was able to rise above his past and reach his potential. He was not to be denied. He composed by listening to his inner music. He composed by listening to himself. His last work was the Ninth Symphony and it was in this symphony that this deaf silent son who knew pain, addiction, and despair included the immortal work "Ode to Joy."

I believe that there is some Beethoven in all silent sons. Inside each of us is a composition lurking right behind the silence. Can you hear yours?

As silent sons we have experienced much pain. Now it's time to work through that pain, learn to let it go, and take our rightful place as healthy men. It's time for potential, not for pain. We know how to be active, forceful, and powerful; now we need to redirect that energy into being healthy. It's time to take responsibility for our lives. We know where we have been and we know what we must do. We know what has happened and that we can't blame it on anyone. We are men who are going to take charge of our lives and determine where we are going.

How do you take control of your own life? In this chapter I identify the ways silent sons I interviewed changed their lives. Regardless of how they did it, they all started by realizing that they wanted to change and that choices for change were available. More importantly, they all knew where change must begin: with themselves.

Dale, age 52, is an office manager. He says, "For most of my life I used this particular problem as an excuse for being an underachiever and feeling sorry for myself. Growing up, I felt I wasn't normal because my home wasn't normal. I felt an emptiness and inadequacy that I tried to fill outside of me. When I got help I started talking about this, and immediately realizing that I wasn't alone helped. Learning how all this affected me and how others dealt with the same thing helped too. But the main thing I had to do was stop using it like an albatross—I had to get on with my life. I had to take responsibility for molding the clay of my life into the shape and substance that I could and wanted to be. I needed to look around and see that everyone has some traumatic or dysfunctional "thing" in their lives, that nobody's life is perfect, that if it hadn't been this, it would have been something else.

Finally, I had to accept the fact that my parents did the best they could. My father learned his behavior from his father, but unfortunately for him he never had the benefit of help. My father never once kissed or hugged me. My father never once gave me a birthday or Christmas present. My father never once told me he loved me. My father instilled paralyzing fear in me by his massive bulk and aggressive, threatening physical presence. My father was very sick and in my heart I am saddened by his seeming lack of love for me, but I know that he was the ultimate loser, not me, and that is equally saddening. He died without ever experiencing the joy, love, or life of his son. He died as he had lived—alone. And that's sad, because it didn't have to be that way. It's so very important to let people know that I care, that I love, and that I am that way today because I choose to be. It means unlearning a lot of behavior. It means being vulnerable and risking pain and rejection. It means saying and doing a lot of things that feel unnatural or foreign. But I realize today that if what I learned was abnormal, then normal behavior will feel foreign for a while even when it is healthy. Yet the choice is mine and only I, with the help of God and others, can break the patterns."

TAKING CONTROL OF YOUR LIFE

No matter how you go about taking control of your life, you, like all silent sons, will be faced with at least four major issues along the way. You will be challenged by your past as it attempts to pull you back into pain. You will need to make peace with yourself in order to have power over your life. You will need to make peace with your family to find lasting inner peace. Finally, you will find freedom and come face-to-face with your potential and be challenged to use it.

MAKING PEACE WITH PAIN AND REALITY

Whether we like it or not, those things that happened to us as boys did happen. As hard as it might be, we must face reality and move on.

> *I have come to realize that I have used my adult relationships and experiences as a stage to play out my unresolved trauma from childhood. I have done whatever I had to do throughout most of my life to escape my feelings because they were too painful to look at. This path of escapism has led me to alcoholism and drug*

addiction which very nearly killed me. In choosing recovery, I have changed my path. I have chosen to face my feelings, and go through the pain, because I have discovered that the only way out is through it.

STAN

It may be hard for you to accept reality, because it carries implications that you might not want to hear or face. Does admitting that you are a silent son imply to you that you are not "all right" because there is something negative about your parents that you would like to hide? Does it suggest that you can't be as successful as you think? Certainly, any and all of these implications can go through your mind.

But you cannot make peace with reality when you deny it. The goal of overcoming denial is to move on. The only thing that can make your past worse is allowing it to negatively affect the present and the rest of your life. When it comes to a painful past, accept it, face it, deal with it—and then get on with it. Keep in mind the following goals to help you make peace with reality and your pain.

· *Assess where you are now.* Assessing yourself means taking a long, hard look at yourself and seeing in what areas you have been affected. It might help to go back over several of the questionnaires you completed in earlier chapters. You need to know your problems in order to handle them. Are you angry; are you still trying to get over how your father treated you; are you having trouble in your relationships, as a parent, or at work? Or are you confused? Maybe the only thing you know is that you don't feel right about certain things in your life. If so, that's a good enough place to start. The key to working through your past begins with honesty.

· *Don't confuse acceptance with approval.* Just because you finally accepted your past doesn't mean that you approve of what happened to you. When we accept our past, we also can accept our accompanying emotions. Reality is a hard thing to deny, but not as hard as the consequences of denial.

· *Stop wanting it to be different.* This is a waste of time. Wishing and wanting for the past to be different keeps you tied to it. You can't change what has happened. But you can change yourself.

· *Let go of the "if only"s.* "If only" statements keep you tied to the past, and tempt you to think you might have done something to ameliorate the dysfunctional situation. You were not in charge of your parents or guardians—it was supposed to be the other way around. "If only" statements keep you second-guessing and looking for answers to the past, when what you should be looking for are answers to your present and future. Change your "if only" statements to "I will" statements. An "I will" statement means you are taking charge of your life now, instead of feeling guilty about things over which you had no control.

· *Stop doing nothing.* Some silent sons do absolutely nothing toward recovering, yet expect things to change. Change means taking action. No change will occur if you don't take an interest in yourself, if you don't share with other men, if you don't seek help, if you don't accept reality, and most importantly, if you don't get any better.

MAKING PEACE WITH YOURSELF AND FINDING POWER

Too many silent sons are internally in pain and try to be externally at peace. But it doesn't work that way. True peace comes from within and begins by learning to like yourself. How can you be at peace with someone you don't like? Of the four stages involved in learning to let go of your past and growing as a man, I believe being at peace with yourself is the most important. Not only is it important for you, but it is an essential prerequisite for being at peace with others. You can't give what you don't have. A man at peace is not easily thrown off balance, because he has power over himself. You know who you are and what you can do. Peace provides inner strength.

Making peace with yourself depends upon your ability to make peace with your feelings. For example, if you are angry, you can't expect to achieve inner peace until you resolve your anger. Your boyhood is over, but its emotional impact remains. Have you kept the hurt locked up, or has it locked you up? Power over yourself means freedom from negative feelings. It means you can stop wasting emotional energy on your past and start using your energy on yourself. It takes energy to learn to let go, but once you have done this you will find the energy necessary to grow. It takes energy to be a healthy man.

The exhausted man is never healthy. He is only tired. How can you be free if you are dragging emotional chains? In order to make peace with yourself and your feelings you will need to learn the following.

· *Treat yourself with respect.* Making peace with yourself leads to self-respect. Throughout this book we have heard many silent sons talk about low self-esteem and not liking who they are. It's time to start liking yourself and giving yourself some respect. Once you begin to respect yourself, you will also expect others to treat you better and you will start believing that you deserve their respect. Treating yourself with respect will require changing some of your negative behaviors. It will mean that you no longer feel compelled to do things that make you uncomfortable or that you don't want to do. It will mean doing things that make you feel good. It will mean saying no to negative demands and yes to yourself. It has taken you years to earn your self-respect. Don't ever give it up again. It isn't for sale and no one can steal it.

· *Let go of your negative feelings.* Negative feelings can keep you from being at peace. They can haunt your soul. Each silent son knows that keeping negative feelings inside leaves less room for inner peace. I have talked with men who have worked through tremendous pain in their lives, but still cannot forgive certain people. No one can tell you to forgive. Each of us must decide how forgiving or not forgiving affects our quest for inner peace. Each of us struggles for peace, but the more negativity we harbor, the harder the struggle becomes.

· *Make peace with all the parts of yourself.* Silent sons are faced not only with the issues of a dysfunctional family, but also with the issues of being men. For most of us these two are closely connected. Don't forget that your dysfunctional issues have also affected many aspects of your male identity. This, too, will require resolution. Don't try to pinpoint just one issue from your past as the key to all your problems. For example, don't assume that just because you forgave your father everything else will automatically be OK. Being a silent son affects every area of your life—and you need to make peace with each and every one of them. If you are trying to gain control over your life, go for all of it.

MAKING PEACE WITH YOUR FAMILY

> *Don't go back to your family and stir up a "hornet's nest."*
>
> MARVIN

Once you have completed the first two stages, you might want to or need to move on to the third stage—trying to make peace with your family. Before you do this, it is important that you have made peace with reality and your pain. Don't skip these stages and start with stage three. Making peace with your family must always be an addition to your own growth, not a substitute for it. Your issues and potential *must* come first.

Making peace with your family can add greatly to your sense of inner peace and resolution over internal conflict. When I speak of family, I include your parents, siblings, spouse/partner, and children, but I believe that trying to make peace with your parents will have the greatest impact on your health. Making peace with your parents does not necessarily mean making peace with the actual people. Each of us has two sets of parents. One set is the parents you carry around inside of you. These are the inner parents. The other set is the real parents. Which set should you make peace with? Try the inner parents first. They are the parents whose emotional impact you are often trying to understand. They are the sources of troubling memories which can stay with you for years after the actual people are long gone.

How do you make peace with your inner or actual parents? By letting go.

A few safe assumptions about parents might help you. First, your parents are not likely to change unless they want to. You cannot wait for this to happen. Second, it is not your job to change them. However, what you can change is your emotional response to them. For example, when you remember certain situations with your parents, what kind of emotional response do you feel? Do you feel anger, rage, hurt, disappointment, or rejection? Or maybe you feel nothing but a sense of loss. Granted, you have no control over what happened. It is done, but you can gain control over how you feel about it today.

And if your parents keep pushing your buttons, learn to retrain your emotional responses. It takes practice, but it can be done. And remember, the reason they can push your buttons so easily is that they installed them!

Making peace with your parents can also create mixed feelings. Obviously, not all dysfunctional parents are dysfunctional all the time. There were probably also good times with your parents. The need to make peace with them does not mean that we have forgotten what they have done for us. We are trying to work through the dysfunctional things to further appreciate the positive ones. In fact, the more positive things you can recall, the easier it will be to make peace.

> *What's helped me was being able to get very angry with my father, even though he died, and then see that he was more than just an alcoholic. Lately, I've been feeling more appreciative of good qualities I have that are similar to his. I've forgiven my father and have grown to love him like I never could when he was alive. Although he was sober for ten years when he died, I wasn't ready to make peace with him until a couple of years ago.*
>
> BUTCH

In order to make peace with your inner or actual parents, try some of the following suggestions, adapted from Harold Bloomfield and Leonard Felder's book *Making Peace with Your Parents.*[2]

- Diffuse guilt.
  Don't feel guilty over what happened. You didn't cause it. You survived it.
- Retrain your emotional habits.
  You can learn new ways of handling old emotions by learning and using new ones. Achieving your potential means using your full range of emotions.
- Understand your parents' childhoods.
  If you want to be better understood for who you are today because of your childhood, then try to learn something about your parents' childhoods in order to better understand them. This will

also make it easier for you to make peace with them. It is easier to handle things we know something about.

• Break free of the approval trap.

Don't waste your time trying to get approval from your parents if you do not approve of them. You're a man and your approval is what counts now.

• Visit without unrealistic expectations.

Don't keep hoping it will be different this time. Be prepared and protect yourself. One of you has to be realistic. How about you?

• Develop your own support family.

You're not the only one. There are many of us, and there are many other people who will share with you. There are people who are more "family" than family will ever be. Use these friends for support and become a friend to them.

• The goal is not to change your parents.

The goal is to change yourself into the kind of man you want to be.

• During changes, you may need to maintain a "safe" distance.

When we are changing, we are also vulnerable because we are taking risk. Protect yourself and know your limits around your parents if they are likely to lead you back into an "emotional relapse."

• Your life first, theirs second.

This doesn't mean you are selfish. It means you can be healthy.

• Be at peace with all of the times that you had.

In my family there were good times and bad. I remember them all. My parents taught me many good things and these things also help me make peace.

ACHIEVING YOUR POTENTIAL

When you make it to this stage, you are ready to fly. You will experience a freedom that you never thought about. An enormous weight will be gone from your shoulders. You will feel energy you thought you never had. One of the most common things I hear from so many men who have made this journey is that they feel reborn. They feel a sense of power and peace about themselves. They have great self-respect. They know they will not be pulled down again. They know they have survived and they know what they can do. You can see it in their faces. They are men of peace, but they are men of power. Do you want to be one of these men? If so, then seize your potential, seize the day, and let yourself fly.

How do you know when you are achieving your potential? You will know because your *life* will be different. I believe that when it comes to recovery or achieving your potential, you *are* your recovery. You either live it or you don't. If you are living up to your potential, you should be doing some of the following things:

- You like yourself.
- You can celebrate yourself and your survival.
- You no longer live in fear.
- You respect yourself and others.
- You have worked through your grief.
- You can handle your memories.
- You can say no.
- You can receive and give love and caring.
- You know where you stand on forgiveness.
- You can trust your emotions.
- You can embrace your masculine spirit.

Achieving your potential is always a journey. It is never a destination. I would be disappointed to grow to a point and then find out that's all there is. For me, each level of growth leads to another level. Each level allows me to feel better about myself and others. Each level allows me to experience and feel things in my life that I had missed and I know other men still miss. When these new levels open up, I find myself thankful for where I have been and for what I have learned, because without these lessons I wouldn't be where I am now. It might have taken me a while to get started, and sure, there were things in my way, but I wouldn't change places with anyone now. There was a time in my life when I would have traded places with anyone because I believed that everyone was better than me. No more.

In this book we have read the stories of so many silent sons and their pain. Many of these men have turned their lives around. When I talked with them they shared several common approaches to healing their lives. All of these silent sons become mentors for us. They will help us by sharing what they know about achieving their potential and putting their pasts behind them. The following are the most common lessons that they offer to us:

1. Join a support group.
2. Establish male relationships.
3. Use spirituality.

JOIN A GROUP

It is difficult and uncomfortable for many of us to ask for help. After all, we still believe that because we are men we can work things out on our own. Have you ever considered that asking for help is a sign of strength too? Don't confuse stubbornness with strength. Reaching out for help gives you strength by allowing you to gain power over your life. Friends who have been there before you will give you strength. Just because you endured most of the pain in your life in silence doesn't mean you have to remain isolated.

I can think of no better place to break down feelings of isolation than in a group. Most silent sons don't need intensive psychotherapy, but we can benefit from sharing our experiences with others and, in many cases, finding out that our feelings are normal. A group also provides a place to try new behaviors.

In addition to finding a group, recovering silent sons emphasized the importance of finding someone they could talk to and trust, such as a mentor or counselor. This may not be easy for you to do, but it is easier than keeping everything inside. If you won't do it, you are letting your pride get in the way of your common sense. Pride has nothing to do with pain, but it can maintain it. Talking with other people and asking for help doesn't make you less of a man. It means you have the sense to realize when you need to ask for support. There are numerous ways to get help and to get support, but none of them will happen if you remain silent. There are a lot of supportive people out there. You need to find them. They will help you, not judge you.

> *Just the support and understanding I get from my group is enough. I mean when you say something and all the other people are shaking their heads like they know those feelings. Now that my wife and I have separated, I really need my group. I'm finally reaching out and they accept me. It's just the acceptance and the warmth you feel that makes these meetings great. The group is my family now.*
>
> JUAN

What kind of group should you join? A healthy one. There are numerous groups out there for silent sons. Look in the yellow pages and you will be surprised at how many different support groups are listed, as well as many different types of men's retreats. Whether you go to a support group or a men's weekend retreat, make sure you have a purpose for going. Set an agenda for yourself about what you hope to gain from the experience. If you go to a group and it wasn't a good experience, don't give up. Try another group. I recommend you try at least five or six different groups before you give up.

The following are some of the characteristics and features which should be present in a healthy support group:[3]

- a shared sense of commitment and cohesiveness
- openness to new members, with older members playing a helper role
- a strong norm of giving help, playing the helper role, evenly distributed throughout the group
- a shared and distributed leadership of various kinds, both formal and informal
- an ideology or rationale that explains the problem the group is addressing and the methodology for coping with it
- a clear sense of purpose to deal with a strong felt need, problem, or illness
- definite traditions and structure
- a strong experiential base

214

- a good balance between the informal, open ethos and the structured dimension related to continuity, group maintenance, and follow-up
- realistic approaches to problems of relapse or regression
- a belief in itself; a belief that the group is effective in dealing with the problems and needs of members
- a relationship with a national organization, although the relationship may be loose and informal

ESTABLISH MALE RELATIONSHIPS

If men ever talk about their problems, it is usually with women. However, we only share with women what we think a man *should* share with women. Whether we are aware of it or not, there is an unspoken line about what we talk about with women that few men will cross. We don't talk about men's issues with women. We don't talk about how it feels to be a man. We can talk a little about our pain or express some emotions, but this is not the same as sharing it all with another man. For most men, sharing emotions or what we are really feeling is a foreign behavior. In the presence of other men we usually keep it to ourselves.

> *Talk with other men. I think it's very important to get involved with other men who are recovering to get a perspective on the "male issues." It's easier and less threatening to talk with women; you don't learn as much about yourself.*
>
> ANDREW

Silent sons who have dealt with many of their issues almost unanimously endorsed talking with other men. Again, this takes courage and the willingness to risk, but the rewards are great. You can casually mention to another man the stress of providing for your family or coming up with the rent or tuition money, and he says sympathetically, "Yeah, tell me about it." Has it ever dawned on you to take the conversation further? Try it. I have had great conversations with women, but I have had my soul touched while talking with men.

You don't need to tell everything to every man—few of us would—but how about opening up to your friend, or finding a mentor? Establishing a relationship with another man means you are willing to find common ground upon which to build your relationship. One form of common ground is sharing with each other what bothers you and talking it through. Have you ever shared a problem with someone, and even if the other person didn't solve it, you still felt better because you discussed it? Talking works.

For years women have known the benefits of talking with other women. As a matter of fact, they started a movement over it many years ago. We are just starting our movement, and it grows from man to man. As men we can support one another by breaking our silence. We can become strong individually and collectively. When we talk with each other a whole new world opens up. It is a world not filled by external masculine domination, but filled with room for the internal issues of men. It is a new world that values what's on the inside of us.

SPIRITUALITY

Spirituality can be defined in many ways and can mean many different things to each of us. For me it has always been a feeling that I am not alone, that there is a sense of purpose in my life, and that I have a "spirit." It is not recovery per se that allows men to change, but rather the *spirit* of recovery. As we discussed earlier, many of us would like to recapture the spirit of our boyhood. Few of us would want our bodies back, but we would like to retain or find again that which was inside us then.

Spirituality is about finding yourself. Spirituality is not religion, although religion can help you find it. It is a feeling that occurs when you realize you are connected with things larger than yourself.

Men who have a strong spirit find balance in themselves. To find this spirit we must often surrender. We must yield our narrow ideas of masculinity, our beliefs that we need no one or anything, and that we are all-powerful. We can still be men and surrender to things that are greater than ourselves without losing our masculinity. We do not lose our inner warrior when we gain spirituality. If anything, we find it.

As I look back over my life, no matter the physical or emotional pain, no matter the level of despair, I know that the one thing that was never broken was my spirit. It was bruised, pushed around, and went into hiding once in a while, but it was never broken. When we have been pounded, it is our spirit that tells us to get up and it is our spirituality that allows us to do it. If the spirit is broken you don't get up. There were days when I went on and I didn't know how I did it, but I knew that I would not be defeated. I knew that my life was going to be better and that I was going to do what it took to get there. My spirit allowed me to maintain balance even when I failed.

I know I said that there is a little bit of the spirit of Beethoven in all silent sons, but I also think there is a little of the boxer "Rocky" in all of us too. In the film, Rocky is a guy who doesn't have much who gets a shot at the heavyweight championship of the world. He gets pounded in the ring, but every now and then he gets in a shot that keeps him in the fight. Finally, in the fourteenth round he is knocked down by the champion, Apollo Creed. His own manager is telling him to stay down. But Rocky won't. His vision blurred, his body wounded, his legs barely able to hold him, he drags himself up. He looks across the ring, not at Apollo Creed, but at life, and motions with his swollen arms, "Come on, come on, I'm not done with you yet."

It didn't matter to Rocky who won the fight. It only mattered to him that at the end he was still standing, and so was his spirit.

But whether it is Beethoven or Rocky, all men have searched for their spirits. Each of us can find ours. Each of us can go the distance. The quest for spirituality is in all men, and in all men there lives an eternal spirit.

I believe that each of us now has a second chance at finding the holy grail, the spirit that allows us to persevere. You had it once as a boy and probably didn't know it. The first time you found it, you stumbled upon it and didn't know what it was. You only realized what you had once it was lost. The second time you find the grail you must earn it, but no matter how much you have to work, the effort will be worthwhile because now you know what it is. It is something that is inside each of us. It is the spirit that will no longer leave you or be denied. Silence has been passed from generation to generation of silent sons and men, but so has the grail. You have a choice, to hold on to your silence or to reach for the grail. You cannot wrap your arms across your chest to hold silence in and reach for the grail at the same time. Open your arms and let the silence fall, never to be embraced again. Reach out, grab the grail, and start a new legend.

AFTERTHOUGHTS

Don't let what you cannot do interfere with what you can do.

JOHN WOODEN

When you were born, you cried and the world rejoiced. Live your life in such a manner that when you die the world cries and you rejoice.

OLD INDIAN SAYING

A man can stand a lot as long as he can stand himself. He can live without hope, without friends, without books, even without music, as long as he can listen to his own thoughts.

AXEL MUNTHE

Never, never, never, never give up.

WINSTON CHURCHILL

I hate quotations.

RALPH WALDO EMERSON

APPENDIX
The Research Behind *Silent Sons*

Silent Sons is based on two related studies of men raised in dysfunctional families conducted by the author. One study involved 126 men who offered written responses to open-ended questions about being raised in various types of dysfunctional families. The topics and quotations in the book are drawn from this "qualitative research." The other study was a quantitative analysis of responses to a survey which was self-administered to two groups of men: 215 self-identified sons of alcoholic families and 206 sons of nonalcoholic families. The statistics in the text are drawn largely from this study.

Another study used in this book involved women. Approximately 100 women who were involved with men from dysfunctional families provided written responses to open-ended questions. These women were either spouses, sisters, mothers, or daughters of silent sons. The topics and quotations in the chapter on women are taken from these interviews.

These complementary studies provide comprehensive descriptions of the experiences of men raised in dysfunctional families. The quantitative data identify the underlying characteristics of silent sons, and the qualitative information shows the problem areas in which these characteristics are manifested or acted out. Most importantly, the studies offer clarification and substantiation of the clinical observations (plus personal anecdotes about men from dysfunctional families) which have heretofore characterized the field.

The tables in this Appendix illustrate some of the findings of the studies and complement the text of *Silent Sons*.

Table 1
Problems Identified by Silent Sons

	Percent	n = 126
Problems for Silent Sons of Dysfunctional Fathers		n = 87
Poor role model	66	
Not worthy of father	44	
Under-fathered	42	
Lack of emotions from father	41	
Fear of being just like him	40	
Problems for Silent Sons of Dysfunctional Mothers		n = 48
Relationships with women	69	
Need to protect and defend mother	40	
Image problems	40	
Trust	33	
Emotional incest	21	
Problems for Silent Sons in Relationships		n = 126
Inability to express emotions	39	
Fear of intimacy	36	
Inability to trust	32	
Fear of inadequacy and rejection	25	
Need to control	23	
Problems for Silent Sons as Parents		n = 92
Fear of repeating mistakes	36	
Lack of parenting skills	36	
Discipline and setting limits	32	
Meeting children's needs	31	
Giving too much	30	

Table 1 *(Continued)*

	Percent	n = 126
Problems for Silent Sons at Work		n = 126
Don't feel good enough	33	
Lack of interpersonal skills	32	
Not a team player	21	
Alcoholism	16	

Note: Percentages equal more than 100 because some men identified more than one problem. "N" means number of people in the study, or represented in this table.

Table 2
Problems with Silent Sons Identified by Women

	Percent	n = 100
Won't let me in	47	
Too much caretaking	36	
Lack of commitment	34	
Project problems onto other women	28	
Don't take care of themselves	22	

Note: Percentages equal more than 100 because some identified more than one problem.

Table 3
Advice from Men about Getting Help

	Percent	n = 126
Join a support group	49	
Establish male relationships	43	
Use spirituality	40	

Note: Percentages equal more than 100 because some identified more than one problem.

Table 4
Adult Sons of Alcoholics versus Adult Sons of Nonalcoholics on Dimensions and Items of the ACOA Index*

	Percent	
	Alcoholic Parent/s (n = 215)	Nonalcoholic Parent/s (n = 206)
Perceived isolation		
What is normal	3.04	2.51†
Feel different from others	3.16	2.71†
Difficulty with intimacy	3.36	2.72†
Inconsistency		
Difficulty following through	2.65	2.43†
Immediate gratification	3.07	2.70†
Manage time poorly	2.74	2.74
Self-condemnation		
Judge self without mercy	3.37	2.81†
Difficulty having fun	3.06	2.50†
Take self very seriously	3.65	3.40†
Control needs		
Overreact to changes	3.16	2.73†
Super responsible or irresponsible	3.40	2.60†
Approval needs		
Seek approval and affirmation	3.37	2.96†
Loyal even when undeserved	3.21	3.03
Lie when easy to tell truth	2.23	1.81†
Rigidity		
Lock self into a course	2.67	2.28†
Seek tension and crisis	2.40	2.05†
Avoid conflict or aggravate it	2.77	2.42†

Table 4 (Continued)

	Percent	
	Alcoholic Parent/s (n = 215)	Nonalcoholic Parent/s (n = 206)
Fear of failure		
Fear rejection and abandonment	2.85	1.87†
Fear criticism and judgment	3.07	2.66†
Fear failure, downgrade success	3.31	2.75†
	60.54	51.68

*Scale: 5 = always, 4 = often, 3 = sometimes, 2 = seldom, 1 = never
†Statistically significant at p ≤ .001.

Table 5
Abuse of Sons in Alcoholic and Nonalcoholic Families

Type of Abuse	Percent	
	Alcoholic (n = 215)	Nonalcoholic (n = 206)
Physical child abuse	25.1	4.0
Child sexual abuse	7.9	1.5
Spouse abuse	32.1	2.5
No abuse existed (includes no neglect or emotional abuse)	19.5	69.8

Notes

Chapter One: Are You a Silent Son?

1. From National Center for Health Statistics, "Monthly Vital Statistics Report," vol. 31, no. 6, Supplement Sept. 30, 1982, U.S. Department of Health and Human Services, p. 7.

Chapter Two: What Kind of Men Are We?

1. Robert Fisher, *The Knight in Rusty Armor* (North Hollywood, Calif.: Wilshire Book Company, 1990).
2. This list of social expectations for men is adapted from John Hough and Marshall Hardy, *Against the Wall: Men's Reality in a Codependent Culture* (Center City, Minn.: Halzelden Foundation, 1991).
3. Robert C. Subby, *Lost in the Shuffle: The Co-Dependent Reality* (Deerfield Beach, Fla.: Health Communications, 1987), p. 15.
4. See Robert J. Ackerman, *Perfect Daughters: Adult Daughters of Alcoholics* (Deerfield Beach, Fla.: Health Communications, 1989).

Chapter Three: Where Do You Stand?

1. Norman Garmezy "Stressors of Childhood," in Norman Garmezy and Michael Rutter, *Stress, Coping, and Development in Children* (New York: McGraw-Hill, 1983), pp. 43–84; Emma Werner, "Resilient Offspring of Alcoholics: A Longitudinal Study from Birth to Age 18," *Journal of Alcohol Studies* (New Brunswick, N.J.: Rutgers University), vol. 47, no. 1, 1986, pp. 34–40.
2. This questionnaire was taken from Matthew McKay, Peter D. Rogers, and Judith McKay, *When Anger Hurts* (Oakland, Calif.: New Harbinger Publications, 1989), pp. 39–40.

Chapter Four: The Dysfunctional Family: The Battle Within

1. Irving L. Janis, *Groupthink* (Boston, Mass.: Houghton Mifflin, 1982).
2. Robert Bly, *Iron John: A Book about Men* (New York: Addison-Wesley, 1990).
3. Nathan W. Ackerman, *The Psychology of Family Life: Diagnosis and Treatment of Family Relationships* (New York: Basic Books, 1958).
4. Margaret Cork, *The Forgotten Children* (Toronto: Addiction Research Foundation, 1969).
5. Robert Bly, Sound editions from Random House audiocassette abridgement of *Iron John* (New York: Random House, 1991).

Chapter Five: Boyhood: Spirit versus Silence

1. Erik H. Erikson, *Childhood and Society* (New York: W. W. Norton, 1963), chapter 7.
2. David Elkind, *The Hurried Child: Growing Up Too Fast Too Soon* (Reading, Mass.: Addison-Wesley, 1981), p. iii.
3. Harris Clemes and Reynold Bean, *How to Raise Children's Self-Esteem*, rev. ed. (San Jose, Calif.: Enrich, 1980), pp. 11–12.
4. Adapted from Sam Keen, *Fire in the Belly: On Being A Man* (New York: Bantam, 1991).
5. Claire Berman, *Adult Children of Divorce* (New York: Simon & Schuster, 1991), p. 20.
6. Avis Brenner, *Helping Children Cope with Stress* (Lexington, Mass.: Lexington Books, 1984).

Chapter Six: Fathers and Sons: Our Fathers Who Art in Us

1. Robert J. Ackerman and Edward W. Gondolf, "Adult Children of Alcoholics: The Effects of Background and Treatment on ACOA Symptoms," *The International Journal of the Addictions,* vol. 26, no. 11, 1991, pp. 1159–1172.
2. John C. Friel, *The Grown Up Man* (Deerfield Beach, Fla.: Health Communications, 1991).

Chapter Seven: Mothers and Sons: Don't Talk about My Mother!

1. Excerpt from *It Doesn't Take a Hero* by General Norman Schwarzkopf in *Newsweek,* September 28, 1992.

2. Robert J. Ackerman, *Let Go and Grow: Recovery for Adult Children* (Deerfield Beach, Fla.: Health Communications, 1987), p. 54.
3. Robert A. Johnson, *He: Understanding Masculine Psychology,* rev. ed. (New York: Harper & Row, 1989).
4. A. C. Acock, D. Baker, and V. L. Bengston, "Mother's Employment and Parent-Youth Similarity," *Journal of Marriage and the Family,* vol. 44, May 1982, pp. 441–55.

Chapter Eight: Relationships: That's the Way I Am

1. Michael E. McGill, *The McGill Report on Male Intimacy* (New York: Harper & Row, 1985), chapter 6.
2. Leo Buscaglia, *Living, Loving and Learning* (New York: Holt, Rinehart & Winston, 1982).
3. McGill, *The McGill Report on Male Intimacy,* pp. 3–31.
4. This questionnaire is adapted from Karen Blaker, *Born to Please: Compliant Women/Controlling Men* (New York: St. Martin's Press, 1988), pp. 32–34.

Chapter Nine: "Are You Listening to Me?" What Women Say about Us

1. This information comes from a questionnaire filled out by more than 6,000 people. The number of women who participated is not indicated by the researchers. The data come from Sam Keen and Ofer Zur as reported in the book *Fire in the Belly: On Being a Man* (New York: Bantam, 1991), p. 256.

Chapter Ten: Parenting: Our Fathers Never Had to Do These Things

1. Margaret Mead, *Male and Female* (New York: Morrow, 1949).
2. L. Hoffman, "Changes in Family Roles, Socialization, and Sex Differences," *American Psychologists,* vol. 32, 1977, pp. 644–58.
3. R. Parke and D. Sawin, "Father-Infant Interaction in the Newborn Period: A Re-evaluation of Some Current Myths," in M. Hetherington and R. Parke, eds., *Contemporary Readings in Child Psychology* (New York: McGraw-Hill, 1981); W. Macky and R. Day, "Some Indicators of Fathering Behaviors in the United States: A Cross-Cultural Examination of Adult Male-Child Interaction," *Journal of Marriage and the Family,* vol. 41, 1979, pp. 287–99.

4. E. E. Lemasters, *Parents in Modern America* (Homewood, Ill.: Dorsey, 1974).
5. Bruce A. Baldwin, "Raising Accountable Kids," *USAir Magazine,* October 1991, pp. 22–31.

Chapter Eleven: Our Jobs: Occupation, Addiction, or Mistress?

Epigraph by Camus from *Barnes & Noble Book of Quotations,* revised and enlarged, Robert I. Fitzhenry, ed. (New York: Harper Perennial, 1987).
1. This questionnaire is adapted from Frank Minirth, *The Workaholic and His Family* (Grand Rapids, Mich.: Baker Book House, 1981), pp. 23–26.
2. Adapted from "Is AA for You?" New York: A. A. World Services, 1973.

Chapter Twelve: Pain, Power, Peace, and Potential

1. Maynard Solomon, *Beethoven* (New York: Schirmer Books, 1977).
2. Harold Bloomfield and Leonard Felder, *Making Peace with Your Parents* (New York: Ballantine, 1985), pp. 56, 94, 120, 169, 188, 208.
3. Adapted from Frank Riessman, "What Makes an Effective Self-Help Group?" *Self Help Reporter,* vol. 6, November/December 1983, p. 27.

Bibliography

Ackerman, Nathan W. *The Psychology of Family Life: Diagnosis and Treatment of Family Relationships*. New York: Basic Books, 1958.

Ackerman, Robert J. *Children of Alcoholics: A Guidebook for Parents, Educators and Therapists*. New York: Simon & Schuster, 1987.

————. *Let Go and Grow: Recovery for Adult Children*. Deerfield Beach, Fla.: Health Communications, 1987.

————. *Perfect Daughters: Adult Daughters of Alcoholics*. Deerfield Beach, Fla.: Health Communications, 1989.

————. *Same House Different Homes: Why Adult Children of Alcoholics Are Not All the Same*. Deerfield Beach, Fla.: Health Communications, 1987.

————, and Edward W. Gondolf. "Adult Children of Alcoholics: The Effects of Background and Treatment on ACOA Symptoms," *The International Journal of the Addictions*, vol. 26, no. 11, 1991, pp. 1159–72.

Acock, A. C., D. Baker, and V. L. Bengtson. "Mother's Employment and Parent-Youth Similarity," *Journal of Marriage and the Family*, vol. 44, May 1982, pp. 441–55.

Baldwin, Bruce A. "Raising Accountable Kids," *USAir Magazine*, October 1991.

Balswick, Jack. *The Inexpressive Male*. Lexington, Mass.: Lexington Books, 1988.

Berman, Claire. *Adult Children of Divorce*. New York: Simon & Schuster, 1991.

Berzon, Betty. *Permanent Partners: Building Gay and Lesbian Relationships That Last*. New York: Penguin Books, 1988.

Bingham, M., et al. *Challenges: A Young Man's Journal for Self-Awareness and Personal Planning*. Santa Barbara, Calif.: Advocacy Press, 1990.

Blaker, Karen. *Born to Please*. New York: St. Martin's Press, 1988.

Bloomfield, Harold, and Leonard Felder. *Making Peace with Your Parents.* New York: Ballantine Books, 1985.

Bly, Robert. *Iron John: A Book about Men.* New York: Addison-Wesley, 1990.

Bolen, Jean Shinoda. *Gods in Everyman: A New Psychology of Men's Lives and Loves.* San Francisco, Calif.: Harper & Row, 1989.

Brenner, Avis. *Helping Children Cope with Stress.* Lexington, Mass.: Lexington Books, 1984.

Buscaglia, Leo. *Living, Loving and Learning.* New York: Holt, Rinehart & Winston, 1982.

Clemes, Harris, and Reynold Bean. *How to Raise Children's Self-Esteem,* rev. ed. San Jose, Calif.: Enrich, 1980.

Cork, Margaret. *The Forgotten Children.* Toronto: Addiction Research Foundation, 1969.

Druck, Ken. *The Secrets Men Keep.* New York: Ballantine Books, 1985.

Elkind, David. *The Hurried Child: Growing Up Too Fast Too Soon.* Reading, Mass.: Addison-Wesley, 1981.

Erikson, Erik H. *Childhood and Society.* New York: W. W. Norton, 1963.

Fine, Reuben. *Troubled Men: The Psychology, Emotional Conflicts and Therapy of Men.* San Francisco, Calif.: Jossey-Bass, 1988.

Finnegan, Dana G., and Emily B. McNally. *Dual Identities: Counseling Chemically Dependent Gay Men and Lesbians.* Center City, Minn.: Halzelden, 1987.

Fisher, Robert. *The Knight in Rusty Armor.* North Hollywood, Calif.: Wilshire Book Co., 1990.

Fossum, Merle. *Catching Fire: Men Coming Alive In Recovery.* San Francisco: Harper & Row, 1989.

Friel, John C. *The Grown Up Man.* Deerfield Beach, Fla.: Health Communications, 1991.

Fulgum, Robert. *All I Really Need to Know I Learned in Kindergarten.* New York: Villard, 1988.

Garmezy, Norman, et al., as reported by Eleanor Hoover in *Human Behavior,* April 1976, pp. 38–42.

Gondolf, Edward W. *Man against Woman: What Every Woman Should Know about Violent Men.* Blue Ridge Summit, Pa.: TAB Books, 1989.

———, and Robert J. Ackerman. "Validity and Reliability of an Adult Children of Alcoholics Index," *The International Journal of the Addictions,* vol. 28, no. 3, 1993, pp. 257–69.

———, and David M. Russell. *Man to Man: A Guide for Men in Abusive Relationships.* Bradenton, Fla.: Human Services Institute, 1987.

Grubman-Black, Stephen D. *Broken Boys/Mending Men: Recovery from Childhood Sexual Abuse*. Blue Ridge Summit, Pa.: TAB Books, 1990.

Hoffman, L. "Changes in Family Roles, Socialization, and Sex Differences," *American Psychologists*, vol. 32, 1977, pp. 644–58.

Hough, John, and Marshall Hardy. *Against the Wall: Men's Reality in a Codependent Culture*. Center City, Minn.: Halzelden Foundation, 1991.

"Is AA For You?" New York: A.A. World Services, Inc., 1973.

Janis, Irving L. *GROUPTHINK*. Boston, Mass.: Houghton Mifflin, 1982.

Johnson, Robert A. *He: Understanding Masculine Psychology*, rev. ed. New York: Harper & Row, 1989.

Keen, Sam. *Fire in the Belly: On Being A Man*. New York: Bantam, 1991.

Lee, John H. *The Flying Boy: Healing the Wounded Man*. Deerfield Beach, Fla.: Health Communications, 1987.

Lemaster, E. E. *Parents In Modern America*. Homewood, Ill.: Dorsey, 1974.

Lenfest, David. *Men Speak Out: In the Heart of Men's Recovery*. Deerfield Beach, Fla.: Health Communications, 1991.

Macky, W., and R. Day. "Some Indicators of Fathering Behaviors in the United States: A Cross Cultural Examination of Adult Male-Child Interaction," *Journal of Marriage and the Family*, vol. 41, 1979, pp. 287–99.

McGill, Michael E. *The McGill Report on Male Intimacy*. New York: Harper & Row, 1985.

McKay, Matthew, et al. *When Anger Hurts*. Oakland, Calif.: New Harbinger Publications, Inc., 1989.

Mead, Margaret. *Male and Female*. New York: Morrow, 1949.

Minirth, Frank. *The Workaholic and His Family*. Grand Rapids, Mich.: Baker Book House, 1981.

Moore, Robert, and Douglas Gillette. *King Warrior Magician Lover: Rediscovering the Archetypes of the Mature Masculine*. San Francisco, Calif.: HarperCollins, 1990.

National Center for Health Statistics, "Monthly Vital Statistics Report," vol. 31, no. 6, Supplement September 30, 1982, U.S. Department of Health and Human Services.

Osherson, Samuel. *Finding Our Fathers*. New York: Fawcett Columbine, 1986.

Parke, R., and D. Sawin. "Father-Infant Interaction in the Newborn Period: A Re-evaluation of Some Current Myths," in M. Hetherington and R. Parke, eds. *Contemporary Readings in Child Psychology*. New York: McGraw-Hill, 1981.

Perrin, Thomas. *I Am an Adult Who Grew Up in an Alcoholic Family*. New York: Continuum, 1991.

Riessman, Frank. "What Makes an Effective Self-Help Group," *Self-Help Reporter,* vol. 6, November/December 1983.

Rubin, Lillian B. *Intimate Strangers: Men and Women Together.* New York: Harper & Row, 1983.

Solomon, Maynard. *Beethoven.* New York: Schirmer Books, 1977.

Subby, Robert. *Lost in the Shuffle.* Deerfield Beach, Fla.: Health Communications, 1987.

Thompson, Keith, ed. *To Be a Man: In Search of the Deep Masculine.* Los Angeles, Calif.: Jeremy P. Tarcher, 1991.

Werner, Emma. "Resilient Offspring of Alcoholics: A Longitudinal Study from Birth to Age 18," *Journal of Alcohol Studies,* vol. 47, no. 1, 1986, pp. 34–40.

Wilson-Schaef, Anne. *When Society Becomes An Addict.* San Francisco, Calif.: Harper & Row, 1987.

Woititz, Janet G. *Adult Children of Alcoholics.* Deerfield Beach, Fla.: Health Communications, 1983.

Acknowledgments

I am deeply grateful to the hundreds of men who have contributed to this book, to those who have helped with the research and interviews, and to the many silent sons who gave me the encouragement to write. I owe you a lot. Additionally, I want to thank the more than 100 women who were willing to be interviewed about silent sons, for their insights and contributions.

To my good friend and colleague, Edward Gondolf, thanks for your endless hours of listening, advising, research assistance, and friendship.

To Kimberly Roth Ackerman, my proofreader, supporter, teammate, and best friend, thanks for believing in me one more time.

To my editors, Fred Hills, Laureen Connelly, Ursula Obst, and Sheila Curry, thanks for helping me put silence into words.